WITH
*Elisabeth
Smith*

# FAST GREEK

**HODDER**
EDUCATION
AN HACHETTE UK COMPANY

For UK order enquiries: please contact
Bookpoint Ltd, 130 Milton Park, Abingdon, Oxon OX14 4SB.
*Telephone:* +44 (0) 1235 827720. Fax: +44 (0) 1235 400454.
Lines are open 09.00–17.00, Monday to Saturday, with a 24-hour
message answering service. Details about our titles and how to
order are available at www.teachyourself.com

For USA order enquiries: please contact McGraw-Hill Customer
Services, PO Box 545, Blacklick, OH 43004-0545, USA.
*Telephone:* 1-800-722-4726. Fax: 1-614-755-5645.

For Canada order enquiries: please contact McGraw-Hill
Ryerson Ltd, 300 Water St, Whitby, Ontario L1N 9B6, Canada.
*Telephone:* 905 430 5000. Fax: 905 430 5020.

Long renowned as the authoritative source for self-guided learning –
with more than 50 million copies sold worldwide – the teach yourself
series includes over 500 titles in the fields of languages, crafts, hobbies,
business, computing and education.

British Library Cataloguing in Publication Data: a catalogue record
for this title is available from the British Library.

Library of Congress Catalog Card Number: on file.

First published in UK 2000 as Teach Yourself Instant Greek
by Hodder Education, part of Hachette UK, 338 Euston Road,
London NW1 3BH.

First published in US 2000 as Teach Yourself Instant Greek by
The McGraw-Hill Companies, Inc.

This edition published 2011.

The **teach yourself** name is a registered trade mark of
Hodder Headline.

Typeset by MPS Limited, a Macmillan Company.

Printed in Great Britain for Hodder Education, an Hachette UK
Company, 338 Euston Road, London NW1 3BH, by CPI Cox &
Wyman, Reading, Berkshire RG1 8EX.

The publisher has used its best endeavours to ensure that the
URLs for external websites referred to in this book are correct and
active at the time of going to press. However, the publisher and
the author have no responsibility for the websites and can make
no guarantee that a site will remain live or that the content will
remain relevant, decent or appropriate.

Hachette UK's policy is to use papers that are natural, renewable
and recyclable products and made from wood grown in sustainable
forests. The logging and manufacturing processes are expected to
conform to the environmental regulations of the country of origin.

Impression number      10 9 8 7 6 5 4 3 2 1
Year                   2014 2013 2012 2011

# Contents

# Read this first

If, like me, you usually skip introductions, don't! Read on! You need to know how **Fast Greek with Elisabeth Smith** works and why. You'll want to know how you are going to speak Greek in just six weeks.

When I decided to write this series I first called it *Barebones*, because that's what you want: no frills, no fuss, just the bare bones and go! So in **Fast Greek with Elisabeth Smith** you'll find:

- Only 451 words to say, well … nearly everything.
- No tricky grammar – just some useful tips.
- No time wasters such as *the pen of my aunt…*
- No phrase book phrases for a working breakfast with the offspring of Onassis
- No need to be perfect. Mistakes won't spoil your success.

I've put some 30 years of teaching experience into this course. I know how people learn. I also know how long they are motivated by a new project before the boredom sets in (a few weeks). And I am well aware how little time they can spare to study each day (about ½ hour). That's why you'll complete **Fast Greek with Elisabeth Smith** in six weeks and get away with 45 minutes a day.

Of course there is some learning to do, but I have tried to make it as much fun as possible. You'll meet Tom and Kate Walker on holiday in Greece. They do the kind of things you need to know about: shopping, eating out and getting about. They chat to the locals, ask a lot of questions and even understand the answers – most of the time! As you will note, Tom and Kate speak Greek all the time, even to each other. What paragons of virtue!

To get the most out of this course, there are only three things you really should do:

- Follow the **Day-by-day guide** as suggested. Please don't skip bits and short-change your success. Everything is there for a reason.

- If you are a complete beginner and have only bought the book, treat yourself to the recording as well. It will help you to speak faster and with confidence.
- Don't skip the next page (**How this book works**). It's essential for your success.

When you have filled in your **Certificate** at the end of the book and can speak **Fast Greek with Elisabeth Smith**, I would like to hear from you. Why not visit my website www.elisabeth-smith.co.uk, e-mail me at elisabeth.smith@hodder.co.uk, or write to me care of Hodder Education, 338 Euston Road, London, NW1 3BH?

And please join me on:

Facebook at www.facebook.com/elisabethsmithlanguages

Twitter at www.twitter.com/LanguagesESmith

*Elizabeth Smith*

# How this book works

**Fast Greek with Elisabeth Smith** has been structured for your rapid success. This is how it works:

**Day-by-day guide** Stick to it. If you miss a day, add one.

**Dialogues** Follow Tom and Kate through Greece. The English of Weeks 1–3 is in 'Greek-speak' to get you tuned in. 'Greek-speak' is English imitating the expressions and word order of Greek: *Not we are on holiday now*. You'll soon get a feel for the language.

**New words** Don't fight them, don't skip them – learn them! The **Flash cards** and the recording will help you. Get your friends or family to test you. Or take the flash cards with you when you are out and about.

**Good news grammar** After you read it you can forget half and still succeed! That's why it's good news.

**Flash words and flash sentences** Read about these building blocks in the **Flash card** section. Then use them! They'll reduce learning time by 50%.

**Learn by heart** Obligatory! Memorizing puts you on the fast track to speaking in full sentences. When you know all six pieces you'll be able to speak in Greek for six minutes without drawing breath.

**Let's speak Greek** You will be doing the talking – in Greek.

**Let's speak more Greek – fast and fluently** Optional extras for more speaking practice without pausing and stumbling.

**Spot the keys** Listen to rapid Greek and make sense of it. Find the key words among a seemingly unintelligible string of sentences and get the gist of what's being said – an essential skill.

**Say it simply** Learn how to use simple Greek to say what you want to say. Don't be shy.

**Test your progress** Mark your own test and be amazed by the result.

**Answers** This is where you'll find the answers to the exercises.

🔊 This icon asks you to switch on the recording.

**Dictionary** Forgotten one of the new words? Look it up in the dictionary.

**Pronunciation** If you don't know about it and don't have the recording go straight to Week 1 **Pronunciation**. You need to know about pronunciation before you can start Week 1.

**Progress chart** Enter your score each week and monitor your progress. Are you going for very good or outstanding?

**Certificate** It's on the last page. In six weeks it will have your name on it.

# Progress chart

At the end of each week record your test score on the progress chart below.

At the end of the course throw out your worst result – anybody can have a bad week – and add up your five best weekly scores. Divide the total by five to get your average score and overall course result. Write your result – *outstanding*, *excellent*, *very good* or *good* – on your **Certificate** at the end of the book.

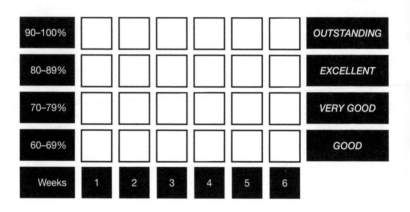

| | | | | | | | |
|---|---|---|---|---|---|---|---|
| 90–100% | | | | | | | OUTSTANDING |
| 80–89% | | | | | | | EXCELLENT |
| 70–79% | | | | | | | VERY GOOD |
| 60–69% | | | | | | | GOOD |
| Weeks | 1 | 2 | 3 | 4 | 5 | 6 | |

Total of five best weeks =

divided by five =

**Your final result _____%**

# Week 1
## Day-by-day guide

Study for 45 minutes a day – or a little longer if you can!

### Day zero
- Start with **Read this first**.
- Read **How this book works**.

### Day one
- Read **In the aeroplane**.
- Listen to/Read **Sto aeroplano**.
- Listen to/Read the **New words**, then learn some of them.

### Day two
- Repeat **Sto aeroplano** and the **New words**.
- Listen to/Read **Pronunciation**.
- Learn more **New words**.

### Day three
- Learn all the **New words** until you know them well.
- Use the **Flash words** to help you.
- Read and learn the **Good news grammar**.

### Day four
- Cut out and learn the **Flash sentences**.
- Listen to/Read **Learn by heart**.

### Day five
- Listen to/Read **Let's speak Greek**.
- Revise! Tomorrow you'll be testing your progress.

### Day six
- Listen to/Read **Let's speak more Greek** (optional).
- Listen to/Read **Let's speak Greek – fast and fluently** (optional).
- Translate **Test your progress**.

### Day seven – This is your day off!

1

# In the aeroplane

Tom and Kate Walker are off to Greece. They board a plane to Skiathos via Athens and squeeze past a fellow passenger sitting in their row. Don't forget that the English of Weeks 1–3 is in 'Greek-speak' to help you get used to the way the language works.

**Tom**    Excuse me, we have the seats 9a and 9b.

**Ari**    Yes, sure, one moment please.

**Tom**    Good morning, we are the Tom and the Kate Walker.

**Ari**    Good morning, I am the Aristotelis.

**Tom**    The Aristotelis Onassis?

**Ari**    No, unfortunately. I am the Aristotelis Nikou.

**Tom**    We go to Skiathos. And you?

**Ari**    No, I am going to Athens. But I am from the Patras.

**Tom**    I was in the Patras in the April. The Patras is very beautiful. I was in the Patras for the company my.

**Ari**    What work do you do?

**Tom**    I work with computer.

**Ari**    And you, Mrs Walker? What do you do? Where (do) you work?

**Kate**    I worked at a school for three years. Now I work at the Rover.

**Ari**    Are you from the London?

**Kate**    No, we are from the Manchester. We were one year in the New York and two years in the London. Now we work in the Birmingham.

**Ari**    I worked for five years at the Fiat. Now I work at the Bank of Greece.

**Tom**    How is the work at the bank? Good?

**Ari**    The work is boring. I work a lot but the money is better. I need a lot of money! I have a big house, a Mercedes and four children. The wife my is American. She has a girlfriend in Florida and she is always on the telephone. It costs a lot.

**Kate**    Now we are on holiday. And you?

**Ari**    Unfortunately no. Not we are on holiday now. We are on holiday the August. Always we go to Porto Rafti but without the children. We have a house there without telephone, and we not have mobile!

# Sto aeroplano

🔊 CD1, tr 2

Tom and Kate Walker are off to Greece. They board a plane to Skiathos via Athens and squeeze past a fellow passenger sitting in their row.

**Tom**  Signomi, exoome tis THesis enea alfa ke enea vita.

**Ari**  Ne, vevea, mia stigmi, parakalo.

**Tom**  Kalimera, imaste o Tom ke i Kate Walker.

**Ari**  Kalimera, ime o Aristotelis.

**Tom**  O Aristotelis Onassis?

**Ari**  Oxi, thistixos. Ime o Aristotelis Nikou.

**Tom**  Pame stin SkiaTHo. Ke esis?

**Ari**  Oxi, pao stin Athina. Ala ime apo tin Patra.

**Tom**  Imoona stin Patra ton Aprilio. I Patra ine poli omorfi. Imoona stin Patra ya tin eteria moo.

**Ari**  Ti thoolia kanete?

**Tom**  Thoolevo me komputer.

**Ari**  Ke esis, kiria Walker? Ti kanete? Poo thoolevete?

**Kate**  Thoolepsa se ena skolio ya tria xronia. Tora thoolevo stin Rover.

**Ari**  Isaste apo to Lonthino?

**Kate**  Oxi, imaste apo to Manchester. Imastan ena xrono stin Nea Iorki ke thio xronia sto Lonthino. Tora thoolevoome sto Birmingham.

**Ari**  Thoolepsa ya pende xronia stin Fiat. Tora thoolevo stin Trapeza tis Elathos.

**Tom**  Pos ine i thoolia stin trapeza? Kali?

**Ari**  I thoolia ine vareti. Thoolevo para poli ala ta lefta ine kalitera. Xriazome pola lefta! Exo ena megalo spiti, mia Mercedes ke tesera pethia. I yineka moo ine Amerikana. Exi mia fili stin Floritha ke ine sinexia sto tilefono. Kostizi poli.

**Kate**  Tora imaste se thiakopes. Ke esis?

**Ari**  Thistixos oxi. Then imaste se thiakopes tora. Imaste se thiakopes ton Avgoosto. Panda pame sto Porto Rafti ala xoris ta pethia. Exoome ena spiti eki xoris tilefono, ke then exoome kinito!

3

# New words

🔊 CD1, tr 3

sto aeroplano *in the aeroplane*
signomi *excuse me*
exoome *we have*
o/i/to/ta/tis/tin/ton *the*
THesi, Thesis *seat, seats*
enea *nine*
alfa, vita *a, b*
ke *and*
ne *yes*
vevea *sure, certain(ly)*
mia stigmi *one moment*
parakalo *please*
kalimera *good morning*
imaste *we are, we were/have been*
ime *I am*
oxi *no*
thistixos *unfortunately*
pame *we/let's go*
sto, stin, stis *to/at/in the*
ke esis *and you?/you, too?*
esis *you*
pao *I go, I'm going*
ala *but*
apo *from*
imoona/imoon *I was*
Aprilio(s) *April*
ine *he/she/it is*
poli *very, much, a lot*
omorfos/i/o *beautiful*
ya *for*
moo *my*
eteria *company/firm*

ti *what*
i thoolia *the work*
kanete *you do/do you do?*
thoolevo *I work*
me *with*
kirios, kiria *Mr/gentleman, Mrs/lady*
poo *where*
thoolevete *you work/do you work?*
thoolepsa *I worked*
se *in, at*
enas/mia/ena *a/one*
skolio *school*
tria *three*
xrono, xronia *year, years*
tora *now*
isaste *you are/are you?*
thio *two*
pende *five*
i Trapeza tis Elathos *the Bank of Greece*
pos *how*
kalos/kali/kalo *good, nice*
varetos/i/o *boring*
poli *a lot,* para poli *too much*
lefta *money*
kalitera *better*
xriazome *I need*
exo *I have*
megalo *big*
spiti *house*
tesera *four*
pethia *children*

yineka *woman, wife*
Amerikana *American*
exi *he/she/it has*
fili *(girl)friend*
sinexia *always*
kostizi *it costs*
se thiakopes *on holiday*

then *not*
Avgoosto *August*
panda *always*
xoris *without*
eki *there*
to tilefono *the telephone*
kinito *mobile phone*

**TOTAL NEW WORDS: 77
... only 293 words to go!**

## Some easy extras
### Mines – *months*
Ianooarios, Fevrooarios, Martios, Aprilios, Maios, Ioonios, Ioolios, Avgoostos, Septemvrios, Oktovrios, Noemvrios, Thekemvrios

### Arithmi – *numbers*

0 = mithen
1 = ena
2 = thio
3 = tria
4 = tesera
5 = pende

6 = eksi
7 = epta
8 = okto
9 = enea
10 = theka

### More greetings
kalispera *good evening*; ya/yasoo (sing)/yasas (pl) *hello, goodbye/ bye*; kalinixta *good night*; adio *goodbye*

5

# Pronunciation

🔊 CD1, tr 4

The Greek language is beautiful, so drop all inhibitions and try to speak Greek rather than English with the words changed. If Greek pronunciation is new to you, buy the recording and listen to the real thing.

As you can see, all the words in **Fast Greek with Elisabeth Smith** have been transliterated into phonetic language. That makes it much easier to learn, especially if you are in a hurry. You don't have to learn the Greek script first but can start speaking straight away.

As Greek is a Mediterranean language the vowels in Greek are similar to Italian or Spanish and are explained below.

## The vowels

The English word in brackets gives you an example of the sound. Say the sound out loud and then the Greek examples out loud.

a *(hat)* Amerik**a**na
e *(yes)* **e**xi
i *(feet)* sp**i**ti
o *(not)* p**o**s
oo *(pool)* thooli**a**

## The consonants

Most consonants are pronounced as in English.

'TH' and 'th' represent two distinct sounds in Greek:

TH as in English *thin* (TH**e**sis *seats*)
th as in English *there* (then **e**xoome *we don't have*)

'x' represents the Greek sound 'kh', similar to, but stronger than, the English '*h*'.

You don't have to think too hard about it all – just go ahead!

## Stress

In this book, the letter in **bold** type tells you to stress the syllable in which it appears, for example, '**e**hume, paraka**lo**, ki**ria**'. Always say the words out loud. That way you'll remember where the accent goes.

When you go to Greece you'll want to know a little of the script, too. So, as an introduction, here's the Greek alphabet. And later in the course there'll also be a few useful flash words in 'real' Greek script, to help you on your way!

A  B  Γ  Δ  E  Z  H  Θ  I  K  Λ  M

α  β  γ  δ  ε  ζ  η  θ  ι  κ  λ  μ

N  Ξ  O  Π  P  Σ  T  Y  Φ  X  Ψ  Ω

ν  ξ  ο  π  ρ  σ,ς  τ  υ  φ  χ  ψ  ω

# Good news grammar

◀) CD1, tr 5

This is the good news part of each week. Remember, I promised: no confusing grammar! I simply explain the differences between Greek and English. This will help you to speak Greek.

## 1 Names of things (nouns)

There are three kinds of noun in Greek: *masculine*, *feminine* and *neuter*.

You can tell which is which by the word 'o', 'i' or 'to' in front of the word.

You can also tell by the ending of the noun:

Most masculine words end in '-os' or '-as':

o yatr**os** (*the doctor*)
o **a**nthras (*the man*)

Most feminine words end in '-a' or '-i':

i thooli**a**, mia stigm**i**

Most neuter words end in '-o' or '-i':

to til**e**fono, to spiti

The adjective describing the noun also ends in '-os' (*masculine*), '-i' (*feminine*) or '-o' (*neuter*). So *the good man, the good work* or *the good house* would be: 'o kal**os a**nthras, i kal**i** thooli**a**, to kal**o** spiti'.

When you talk about more than one thing (plural) 'o, i, to' change into 'i, i, ta' and the endings of the nouns also change, to '-i', '-es' or '-a'.

   *Example*: i kal**i a**nthres, i kal**es** thooli**es**, ta kal**a** spitia.

This is beginning to sound very complicated, and I don't expect you to learn it or remember it all. You'll pick it up as you go along, without even noticing it! And the best news is, if you muddle things up and make a mistake and say: 'to kal**a** spitia' or 'o kal**i a**nthres', people will not throw a fit but still understand you perfectly well!

## 2 Doing things (verbs)

Unlike the English, Greeks do not use the *I, you, he, she, it, we* or *they* persons, to identify who is doing something unless they wish to clarify or stress it. So the only way you can tell who it is that is doing something is from the verb itself. Each person has his, her or its own verb form and ending. Occasionally a verb ending is shared which could lead to some confusion, but amazingly enough it works out all right once it's in a sentence.

There are a few verbs which you'll use every day. I have put the first two of these into a box below. Learn them now until you can say them with your eyes closed. It won't take long!

| **to be** | |
|---|---|
| i**me** | *I am* |
| i**saste** | *you are* |
| i**ne** | *he/she/it is* |
| i**maste** | *we are* |
| i**ne** | *they are* |

| **to have** | |
|---|---|
| e**xo** | *I have* |
| e**xete** | *you have* |
| e**xi** | *he/she/it has* |
| e**xoome** | *we have* |
| e**xoone** | *they have* |

## 3 The Tom, the Kate, the company my

Did you notice? An extra *the* keeps on popping up everywhere in front of nouns and names: 'Imaste **o** Tom ke **i** Kate Walker' (*We are the Tom and the Kate Walker*).

When you want to say: *for my company*, you can't just say literally 'ya moo eteria'. As you will see in the following section, you have to shuffle things around – adding *the* in front of the noun and putting *my* after the noun – and say:

ya **tin** eteria **moo**: *for the company my*

Sounds rather grand doesn't it?... 'o Charles; o komputer moo.'

### Moo, sas, too, tis

When Greeks say *my*, *your*, *his*, *her*, they always add 'o', 'i' or 'to' depending on whether the word which follows is masculine (male), feminine (female) or neuter (neither male nor female).

So as well as 'o komputer moo', they say 'i efimeritha moo' (*my newspaper*), and 'to aftokinito too' (*his car*).

## 4 Two into one

Greeks love their language to be as smooth as possible. Little pairs of words like *to the* sound too 'staccato' to them so they 'melt' the two words into one. Here are three examples:

se + to = sto se + **t**on = ston se + **t**in = stin

And if you don't 'melt'? No problem. People will still understand you.

There are three forms of the Greek for '*in (the)*', depending on the gender of the city name in Greek:

ston Volo (*Volos* is masculine)
stin Nea Yorki (*New York* is feminine)
sto Parisi (*Paris* is neuter)

# Learn by heart

🔊 CD1, tr 6

Don't be tempted to skip this exercise because it reminds you of school… If you want to speak, not stumble, saying a few lines by heart does the trick!

Learn **Kalimera** by heart after you have filled in the gaps with your personal, or any, information. Say **Kalimera** out loud and fairly fast. Can you beat 40 seconds?

---

**Kalimera**

Kalimera, ime o/i .............................................................................
(*name*)

Ime apo to(n)/ti(n) ............................................................(*place*)

Imoona sto .........................(*place*) ton ...................................(*month*)

Thoolepsa ya tin ...................................................(*firm*) ya thio xronia.

Tora thoolevo stin .......................................................................(*place*)

Exo ena megalo spiti stin/sto ...............................(*place*). Kostizi poli.

Ton Avgoosto pame stin/sto .......................................................(*place*).

Pos ine i ATHina ton Aprilio? Omorfi?.....................................................

---

**11**

# Let's speak Greek

◀》 CD1, tr 7

Here are ten English sentences. Read each sentence and say it in Greek – out loud. Check your answer opposite before you try the next sentence. You can also check your answers on the recording.

1 Are you from London?
2 Yes, I am from London.
3 I am on holiday in August.
4 We are going to Corfu *(Kerkira)*.
5 I was in Athens for my firm.
6 Do you have a Ferrari?
7 No – unfortunately!
8 We have a house in Athens.
9 How is the job with Fiat, good?
10 No, it is boring, but the money is better.

Well, how many did you get right? If you are not happy do it again. Here are some questions in Greek. Answer them in Greek. Start every answer with 'Ne', and talk about yourself.

11 Isaste apo to Manchester?
12 Exete spiti sto Lonthino?
13 Pame stin Kerkira. Ke esis?
14 Thoolevete stin Trapeza tis Elathos?
15 Exete kali thoolia?

Now tell someone in Greek…

16 …that you have two children.
17 …that you were in Athens.
18 …that you have a Fiat Uno.
19 …that you are going to Skiathos.
20 …that Birmingham is boring in November.

## Answers

1 Isaste apo to Lonthino?
2 Ne, ime apo to Lonthino.
3 Ime se thiakopes ton Avgoosto.
4 Pame stin Kerkira.
5 Imoona stin ATHina ya tin eteria moo.
6 Exete mia Ferrari?
7 Oxi – thistixos!
8 Exoome ena spiti stin ATHina.
9 Pos ine i thoolia me tin Fiat, kali?
10 Oxi, ine vareti, ala ta lefta ine kalitera.
11 Ne, ime apo to Manchester.
12 Ne, exo spiti sto Lonthino.
13 Ne, ke ego pao stin Kerkira.
14 Ne, thoolevo ya tin Trapeza tis Elathos.
15 Ne, exo kali thoolia.
16 Exo thio pethia.
17 Imoona stin ATHina.
18 Exo ena Fiat Uno.
19 Pao stin SkiaTHO.
20 To Birmingham ine vareto ton Noemvrio.

Well, what was your score? If you had more than 18 correct answers you can give yourself a big pat on the back.

# Let's speak more Greek

🔊 CD1, tr 8

Here are some optional exercises. They may stretch the 45 minutes a day by 15 minutes. But the extra practice will be worth it.

And always remember: near enough is good enough!

## In your own words

This exercise will teach you to express yourself freely. Use only the words you have learned so far.

Tell me in your own words that…

*Example: you are Peter Smith*
Ime o Peter Smith.

1 you are from Manchester
2 you have an American (female) friend
3 you are a workaholic…
4 …but you don't have a lot of cash
5 you have two children
6 the children are six and eight
7 unfortunately you work with PCs; the work is not interesting
8 your wife spends a lot of time on the phone
9 you own a property in Athens
10 you are on holiday without the children

---

## Answers

1 Ime apo to Manchester.
2 Exo mia fili Amerikana.
3 Thoolevo sinexia…/Thoolevo para poli…
4 …ala then exo pola lefta.
5 Exo/exoome thio pethia.
6 Ta pethia ine eksi ke okto.
7 Thistixos thoolevo me komputer. I thoolia ine vareti.
8 I yineka moo ine sinexia sto tilefono.
9 Exo/exume ena spiti stin ATHina.

10 Ime/Imaste se thiakopes xoris ta pethia.

# Let's speak Greek – fast and fluently

🔊 CD1, tr 9

No more stuttering and stumbling. Get out the stopwatch and time yourself with this fluency practice. Translate each section and check if it is correct, then cover up the answers and say the three or four sentences fast! Try to say them in 20 seconds. Some of the English is in 'Greek-speak' to help you.

*Good evening. I am going to Athens. You, too?*
*No, I work in Patras – for a bank. But I am going to Skiathos.*
*I am on holiday – without computer.*

Kalispera. Pao stin ATHina. Ke esis?
Oxi, thoolevo stin Patra – ya mia trapeza. Ala pao stin SkiaTHo.
Ime se thiakopes – xoris komputer.

*How is Skiathos? Is it big?*
*No, it is not big, but it is not boring.*
*It is very beautiful in June.*
*A house in Skiathos costs a lot of money.*

Pos ine i SkiaTHos? Ine megali?
Oxi, then ine megali, ala then ine vareti.
Ine poli omorfi ton Ioonio.
Ena spiti stin SkiaTHo kostizi pola lefta.

*I have a girlfriend, (the) Nana.*
*She has a house in Athens.*
*Oh, excuse me. One moment, please, it is (the) Nana.*
*She is always on the phone. Bye!*

Exo mia fili, tin Nana.
Exi ena spiti stin ATHina.
O, signomi. Mia stigmi, parakalo, ine i Nana.
Ine panda sto tilefono. Yiasas!

# Test your progress

This is your only written exercise. You'll be amazed at how easy it is. Translate the 20 sentences without looking at the previous pages.

Don't try to show the stress/accent when you write. That would take you forever!

1 Good morning, we are Ari and Jane.
2 I am from Athens, and you?
3 Where (do) you work now?
4 I was in Athens in October.
5 My girlfriend is in Greece for one year.
6 We always go to Rhodes (Rotho) in June.
7 I worked at Fiat in May.
8 What (do) you do in London?
9 I work in a school.
10 The big house in Porto Rafti is for the children.
11 One moment please, where is Aristotelis?
12 (Does) the house have a telephone? No, unfortunately (not).
13 (Does) a Ferrari cost a lot? Yes, sure, it costs too much.
14 How is the work in Greece, good?
15 Aristotelis has a girlfriend in my firm.
16 We have been in Skiathos for three days.
17 We have good seats in (the) aeroplane.
18 I always have boring holidays.
19 He has a beautiful wife, a Lamborghini and a lot of money.
20 Are you (the) Mrs Onassis? You have a big aeroplane.

When you have finished, look up the answers in the **Answers** section and mark your work. Then enter your result on the **Progress Chart** at the front of the book. If your score is higher than 80% you'll have done very well indeed.

# Week 2

## Day-by-day guide

45 minutes a day – but a little extra will step up your progress!

### Day one

- Read **In Koukounaries**.
- Listen to/Read **Stis Koukounaries**.
- Listen to/Read the **New words**. Learn 20 easy ones.

### Day two

- Repeat **Stis Koukounaries** and the **New words**.
- Learn the harder **New words**.
- Use the **Flash words** to help you.

### Day three

- Learn all the **New words** until you know them well.
- Read and learn the **Good news grammar**.

### Day four

- Cut out and learn the **Flash sentences**.
- Listen to/Read **Learn by heart**.

### Day five

- Listen to/Read **Let's speak Greek**.
- Go over **Learn by heart**.

### Day six

- Listen to/Read **Let's speak more Greek** (optional).
- Listen to/Read **Let's speak Greek – fast and fluently** (optional).
- Translate **Test your progress**.

### Day seven – This is a study-free day!

# In Koukounaries

In Skiathos Tom and Kate hire a car and drive to Koukounaries.
They book into a hotel for the night and then look for somewhere to
have a drink.

**Kate**      Good morning. (Do) you have a double room for one night,
            and no(t) too expensive?

**Hotelier**  Yes, we have a double room, a little small, with bath and shower.
            The shower doesn't work, maybe the husband my is able to it fix.

**Tom**       Where is the room?

**Hotelier**  It is here, left. Is it enough big?

**Tom**       It is a little small, but not bad. How much (does) it cost?

**Hotelier**  Only 100 euros for two, but no credit cards! The breakfast is
            from the eight until nine and half.

**Tom**       OK. We'll take it. But are we able to have breakfast at eight
            less quarter? Tomorrow at eight and quarter we want to go
            to the Axlathies.

**Kate**      Excuse me, where can we to drink something? Is there
            a bar here near?

**Hotelier**  There are two bars five minutes from here. It is not difficult.
            Thirty metres right and then straight on.

*(In the bar...)*

**Waiter**    What do you want?

**Kate**      We want a coffee and a tea with milk.

**Waiter**    (Do) you want something to eat?

**Tom**       What (do) you have?

**Waiter**    We have apple pie or bread rolls.

**Kate**      Two bread rolls with ham, please.

**Tom**       The ham not is good.

**Kate**      The ham my is very good.

**Tom**       The table is very small.

**Kate**      But the toilet is big and very clean.

**Tom**       The tea is cold.

**Kate**      But the waiter is handsome.

**Tom**       Waiter! The bill, please!

**Waiter**    15 euros, please.

# Stis Koukounaries

🔊 CD1, tr 10

In Skiathos Tom and Kate hire a car and drive to Koukounaries.
They book into a hotel for the night and then look for somewhere to
have a drink.

**Kate**      Kalimera. Exete ena thiklino ya mia nixta, ke oxi poli
akrivo?

**Hotelier**  Ne, exoome ena thiklino, ligo mikro, me banio ke doosh. To
doosh then thoolevi, isos o anthras moo bori na to ftiaksi.

**Tom**       Poo ine to thomatio?

**Hotelier**  Ine etho, aristera. Ine arketa megalo?

**Tom**       Ine ligo mikro, ala oxi asximo. Poso kostizi?

**Hotelier**  Mono ekato evro ya thio, ala oxi pistotikes kartes!
To proino ine apo tis okto mexri tis enea ke misi.

**Tom**       Endaksi. To pernoome. Ala boroome na exoome proino stis
okto para tetarto? Avrio stis okto ke tetarto theloome na
pame stis Axlathies.

**Kate**      Signomi, poo boroome na pioome kati? Exi kanena bar etho
konda?

**Hotelier**  Ine thio bar pende lepta apo etho. Then ine thiskolo. Trianda
metra theksia ke meta isia.

*(Sto bar...)*

**Waiter**    Ti THelete?

**Kate**      THeloome enan kafe ke ena tsai me gala.

**Waiter**    THelete kati na fate?

**Tom**       Ti exete?

**Waiter**    Exoome milopita i psomakia.

**Kate**      Thio psomakia me zambon, parakalo.

**Tom**       To zambon then ine kalo.

**Kate**      To zambon moo ine poli kalo.

**Tom**       To trapezi ine poli mikro.

**Kate**      Ala i tooaleta ine megali ke poli kaTHari.

**Tom**       To tsai ine krio.

**Kate**      Ala o servitoros ine omorfos.

**Tom**       Servitore! Ton logariasmo, parakalo!

**Waiter**    Thekapende evro, parakalo.                **19**

# New words

🔊 CD1, tr 11

Learning words the traditional way can be boring. If you enjoyed the flash cards why not make your own for the rest of the words. Always say the word out loud. It's the fast track to speaking!

thomatio *room*
thiklino *double room*
i nixta *the night*
akrivo *expensive*
ligo *little*
mikros/i/o *small*
banio *bath*
doosh *shower*
isos *perhaps*
anthras *husband/man*
bori (na ftiaksi…) *he/she/it can (fix…)*
etho *here*
aristera *left*
arketa *enough*
oxi asximo/a *not bad*
poso kostizi *how much does it cost?*
mono *only*
ekato *(a) hundred*
evro *euro, euros*
pistotikes kartes *credit cards*
proino *breakfast*
mexri *until*
miso/misi *half*
endaksi *OK*
pernoome *we take*
boroome (na) *we can*
(na) exoome proino *(to) have breakfast (we)*
para *less/before (with time)*
ke *and/past (with time)*
tetarto *quarter*

avrio *tomorrow*
THeloome (na) *we want/we'd like*
pioome *drink (we)*
kati *something*
kanena *none/any (things)*
konda *near*
lepto/lepta *minute, minutes*
thiskolos/i/o *difficult*
trianda *30*
metra *metres*
theksia *right*
meta *then*
isia *straight on*
sto bar *in the bar*
ti THelete? *what would you like? (lit. what (do) you want?)*
kafes/kafe *coffee*
tsai *tea*
gala *milk*
kati na fate *something to eat*
milopita *apple pie*
i *or*
psomaki, psomakia *bread roll/ rolls (little/small bread)*
zambon *ham*
trapezi *table*
i tooaleta, tooaletes *the toilet(s)*
kaTHaros/i/o *clean*
krios/a/o *cold*
servitoros *waiter*
logariasmos *bill*
thekapende *15*

> **TOTAL NEW WORDS: 60**
> …only 233 words to go!

## Some useful extras

### Arithmi – *more numbers*

| | | |
|---|---|---|
| *11* entheka | *19* thekaenea | *60* eksinda |
| *12* thotheka | *20* ikosi | *70* evthominda |
| *13* thekatria | *21* ikosiena | *80* ogthonda |
| *14* thekatesera | *22* ikosithio | *90* eneninda |
| *15* thekapende | *23* ikositria | *100* ekato |
| *16* thekaeksi | *30* trianda | *200* thiakosia |
| *17* thekaepta | *40* saranda | *1000* xilia |
| *18* thekaokto | *50* peninda | |

### I ora – *the time*

| | |
|---|---|
| ti ora? | *at what time?* |
| stis pende? | *at five o'clock?* |
| ine mia | *it's one o'clock* |
| ine thio | *it's two o'clock* |
| ena lepto | *a minute (just a minute)* |
| ke misi | *half past* |
| ke tetarto | *quarter past* |
| mia ora | *an hour* |
| mia mera | *a day* |
| mia evthomatha | *a week* |
| enas minas | *a month* |
| enas xronos | *a year* |
| too xronoo | *next year* |
| para tetarto | *quarter to* |

# Good news grammar

🔊 CD2, tr 12

## 1 I, you, he/she/it, we, they

In Greek these are:

ego
esis
aftos/afti/afto
emis
afti

As you know, they are only used for emphasis: *I do this, **you** did that*.

Although there is no particular way to know immediately whether 'afti' on its own means *she* or *they*, when it is used in a sentence, it becomes obvious.

'Esis' is the formal and polite way of saying *you*. You use it when you are talking to someone you don't know, someone in authority, and more than one person. When in Greece always use 'esis'. There is also 'esi' for family and friends but that needs a lot more grammar. Leave that till next year.

## 2 Saying *then* ('not')

Did you notice in Week 1 what happened to the *not* when o Ari Nikou said: 'Then imaste se thiakopes tora?' (***not** we are on holiday now*). The *not* moved in front of the verb. It does this all the time:

> I thoolia ine kali. I thoolia then ine kali.
> *The work is good. The work not is good.*

## 3 Verbs (again)

This week's good news: two more everyday verbs – *go* and *can* – for easy learning. You'll need only a few minutes this time, because there is a bit of a pattern to each verb:

*I* usually ends in '-o': '**ex**o, k**an**o, th**oo**lev**o**'
*You* ends in '-ete' (or '-ite'): '**ex**ete, k**an**ete, th**oo**lev**ete**, bor**ite**'
*He/she/it* ends in '-i': '**ex**i, k**an**i, th**oo**lev**i**'
*We* ends in '-oome': '**ex**oome, k**an**oome, th**oo**lev**oome**'
*They* ends in '-oon' or '-oone': '**ex**oon(e), k**an**oon(e), th**oo**lev**oon(e)**'

Here's an example: **kano** *(I do)*.

| *I* | *you* | *he/she/it* | *we* | *they* |
|------|--------|-------------|---------|------------|
| kano | kanete | kani | kanoome | kanoon(e) |

There are a total of 30 verbs in **Fast Greek with Elisabeth Smith** and 21 of these are 'regular', which means they follow the above pattern.

That leaves you with nine 'rebels' – verbs which make their own rules. You have learnt two rebels already – '**exo**' and '**ime**' *have* and *be*. Here's one more: '**pao**' *(go)*. Then there's '**boro**' *(can)* – a useful fellow and member of the good verbs group.

Spend five minutes on each.

| pao | *I go* |
|------|----------|
| pate | *you go* |
| pai | *he/she/it goes* |
| pame | *we go* |
| pane | *they go* |

| bor**o** (na) | *I can* |
|----------------|-----------------|
| bor**ite** (na) | *you can* |
| bor**i** (na) | *he/she/it can* |
| bor**oo**me (na) | *we can* |
| bor**oo**ne (na) | *they can* |

## 4 A recap

While you are in the swing of things let's recap on the rest of the regular verbs which you have learnt so far. Once you know how to say *I ... work/fix/take/drink/want (would like)*, you know the pattern, and you can say the rest.

Now take these five on board, too:

thool**e**vo – fti**a**xno – p**e**rno – p**i**no – TH**e**lo

## 5 A bonus

In Greek the same verbs are used for whether it's an action you do or an action you are doing. Therefore *I go* and *I am going* would be: '**pa**o' and '**pa**o'. That makes things a lot simpler.

# Let's speak Greek

🔊 CD1, tr 13

Now let's practise what you have learnt. Here are ten English sentences for you to say in Greek out loud! After each sentence check to see if you got it right. If you didn't, do the exercise again.

1 We would like a room.
2 At what time is there breakfast?
3 The telephone does not work.
4 How much is (costs) the room?
5 Where is the bar, on the right or on the left?
6 Is there (do you have) something to eat?
7 All right, we take it.
8 Can we go to Athens?
9 We would like to go at half past two.
10 Excuse me, the bill, please.

Now answer in Greek. Use 'ne' and speak about yourself.

11 Thoolevete stis okto ke misi?
12 THelete ena psomaki?
13 Exete pola lefta?

Now answer with 'oxi' and speak for yourself and a friend.

14 Exete ena trapezi ya pende?
15 Exete peninda evro?
16 Exete tsai me gala?

And now answer freely. Your answers may differ from mine but still be correct.

17 Poo ine to ksenothoxio (*hotel*) Aliki?
18 Poo ine to thomatio?
19 Poo ine to bar?
20 Poso kostizi to tilefono?

## Answers

1 THeloome ena thomatio.
2 Ti ora ine to proino?
3 To tilefono then thoolevi.
4 Poso kostizi to thomatio?
5 Poo ine to bar, theksia i aristera?
6 Exete kati na fame?
7 Endaksi, to pernoome.
8 Boroome na pame stin ATHina?
9 THeloome na pame stis thio ke misi.
10 Signomi, ton logariasmo, parakalo.
11 Ne, thoolevo stis okto ke misi.
12 Ne, THelo ena psomaki.
13 Ne, exo pola lefta.
14 Oxi, then exoome ena trapezi ya pende.
15 Oxi, then exoome peninda evro.
16 Oxi, then exoome tsai me gala.
17 To ksenothoxio Aliki ine stin Patra.
18 Ine theksia ke meta isia.
19 Ine isia ke meta aristera.
20 Kostizi para poli.

# Let's speak more Greek

Here are the two optional exercises. Remember, they may stretch the
45 minutes a day by 15 minutes. But the extra practice will be worth it.

## In your own words

This exercise will teach you to express yourself freely. Use only the
words you have learned so far. Ask me in your own words...

1 if an ensuite double room is available
2 what the price of the room is for one night
3 where you can have a coffee

Tell me...

4 that there is a bar at 20 minutes from here, straight ahead
5 you would like breakfast at 7.30
6 you are thinking of going to Corfu tomorrow
7 you want one coffee and apple pie
8 what you don't like about the café (the table is too small and the
   ham isn't good)
9 what Kate likes about the café (the toilets are clean and the waiter is
   very handsome)
10 that the bill is € 9.60

## Answers

1 Signomi. Exete ena thiklino me banio?
2 Poso kostizi to thomatio ya mia nixta?
3 Poo boroome na pioome enan kafe?
4 Exi ena bar ikosi lepta apo etho, isia.
5 THeloome to proino stis efta ke misi.
6 THeloome na pame stin Kerkira avrio.
7 THeloome enan kafe ke mia milopita.
8 Then ine kala etho. To trapezi ine poli mikro ke to zambon then ine
   kalo.
9 I Kate lei: Ine kala etho. I tooaletes ine kaTHares ke o servitoros ine
   omorfos.
10 O logariasmos ine enea evro ke eksinda lepta.

# Let's speak Greek – fast and fluently

🔊 CD1, tr 15

No more stuttering and stumbling! Get out the stopwatch and time yourself with this fluency practice.

Translate each section and check if it is correct, then cover up the answers and say the three or four sentences fast! Try to say them in 20 seconds.

*Good evening, do you have a room with bath?*
*80 euros is a little expensive.*
*We take a double room with shower.*
*How much is the breakfast? Can we have breakfast at 7 o'clock?*

Kalispera. **E**xete **e**na thom**a**tio me b**a**nio?
Ogth**o**nda evr**o** **i**ne l**i**go akriv**o**.
Pern**oo**me **e**na thikl**i**no me d**oo**sh.
P**o**so kost**i**zi to proin**o**? Bor**oo**me na **e**x**oo**me proin**o** stis ept**a**?

*Where is my house? Straight on, then 50 metres right.*
*But we are going tomorrow to Patras.*
*We would like to go at half past nine.*

P**oo** **i**ne to sp**i**ti m**oo**? **I**sia, met**a** pen**i**nda m**e**tra theks**i**a.
Al**a** **a**vrio p**a**me stin P**a**tra.
TH**e**l**oo**me na p**a**me stis en**e**a ke m**i**si.

*The bar here is very small and very expensive.*
*But the coffee is good, and the rolls with ham are not bad.*
*The bill, please. How much? 30 euros for one coffee and two rolls?*
*We do not have enough money!*

To bar eth**o** **i**ne pol**i** mikr**o** ke pol**i** akriv**o**.
Al**a** o kaf**e**s ine kal**o**s, ke ta psom**a**kia me zamb**o**n then **i**ne **a**sxima.
Ton logariasm**o**, parakal**o**. P**o**so? Tri**a**nda evr**o** ya **e**nan kaf**e**
ke th**i**o psom**a**kia?
Then **e**x**oo**me arket**a** l**e**fta.

# Learn by heart

🔊 CD1, tr 16

Learn the eight lines Then exo pola lefta... by heart. Try to say them with a bit of 'drama' in 40 seconds! Choose one of these to fill the gap: 'o anthras moo, i yineka moo, o filos *(male friend)* moo, i fili moo'. But here you need to change these words to: 'ton anthra moo, tin yineka moo, ton filo moo, tin fili moo'.

---

**Then exo pola lefta...**

Then exo pola lefta ala THelo*/THeloome na pao/pame thiakopes me...

THeloome na pame stin ATHina me to Rover.

Ine poli omorfi ton Aprilio.

To ksenothoxio** Pavlithi then ine poli akrivo.

Poso kostizi?

Mono ekato evro tin nixta.

Boroome na pame? Oxi.

Panda exi poli thoolia ke to Rover then thoolevi.

*thelo: *I would like* **ksenothoxio: *hotel*

---

# Test your progress

Translate the following sentences in writing. What do you remember without looking back?

1 Where is (there) a telephone?
2 Excuse me, we only have credit cards.
3 Can we go at seven tomorrow?
4 Do you have (a) enough big table? We are five.
5 The small rooms do not have (a) bath.
6 We would like to eat ham and rolls.
7 We can go from (the) six to (the) quarter to seven.
8 Where can we drink something here near?
9 We were in the bar from nine to half past ten.
10 All right, we take the Rover for a day.
11 How much does the breakfast cost? Only 10 euros.
12 What (do) you want? The computer? It is not working.
13 How is the apple pie? Good but expensive?
14 Where are the toilets, on the left or on the right?
15 I can go to Hollywood.
16 A coffee, please… we drink too much coffee!
17 Where is (the) Mrs Pavlithi? Perhaps in the bar?
18 Six euros for a cold tea? It is a little expensive!
19 I was in Rhodes in February. It is not bad.
20 There are 300 bars here, one is (at) 30 metres on the right.

Check your answers. The **Progress chart** awaits your score.

# Week 3

## Day-by-day guide

Study for 45 minutes a day – but there are no penalties for doing more!

### Day one

- Read **Let's go shopping**.
- Listen to/Read **Pame ya psonia**.
- Listen to/Read the **New words**, then learn some of them.

### Day two

- Repeat **Pame ya psonia** and the **New words**.
- Learn all the **New words**. Use the **Flash cards**!

### Day three

- Test yourself on all the **New words** – boring, boring, but you are over half-way already!
- Listen to/Read **Spot the keys**.
- Learn the **Good news grammar**.

### Day four

- Go over the **Good news grammar**.
- Cut out and learn the ten **Flash sentences**.

### Day five

- Listen to/Read **Let's speak Greek**.
- Listen to/Read **Learn by heart**.

### Day six

- Listen to/Read **Let's speak more Greek** (optional).
- Listen to/Read **Let's speak Greek – fast and fluently** (optional).
- Go over **Learn by heart**.
- Have a quick look at the **New words**, weeks 1–3.
- You now know over 200 words! Well, more or less.
- Translate **Test your progress**.

### Day seven – Enjoy your day off!

# Let's go shopping

Tom and Kate have rented a holiday apartment for a week near Athens. Kate plans to do some shopping, but Tom has other ideas…

**Kate**   Today we must do the shopping. Let's go into the centre with the bus.

**Tom**   But there is bad weather, it makes cold and there is a lot of sport on television – the golf at two and a half.

**Kate**   I am sorry, but we must go first to the cashpoint machine and to the post office or kiosk for stamps… then to the chemist's and to the dry cleaner's.

**Tom**   In that case, no golf… perhaps the football at four and a quarter. This is all?

**Kate**   No, we have to go to a department store to buy a new suitcase. Then I have to go to the supermarket and to the hairdresser's. And afterwards I want to buy shoes.

**Tom**   Good grief! Until when are the shops open?

**Kate**   Until the seven and half, I believe.

**Tom**   Then no football… perhaps the tennis at the eight.

(Later…)

**Kate**   Hello Tom, here is the shopping: 200g ham, a piece cheese, half a kilo apples, two kilos potatoes, feta cheese, sugar, bread, butter, some eggs, six beers and a bottle (of) wine. I have bought too many things.

**Tom**   It doesn't matter. Yesterday we not ate much. And what is in the big bag? Something for me?

**Kate**   Well, near to the Notos Galleries there was a small shop and I saw some shoes which were the number (size) my. Not are they beautiful? White and blue. The sales assistant was very nice and handsome like the Tom Cruise.

**Tom**   Who is the Tom Cruise? And how much cost the shoes?

**Kate**   They were a little expensive, but they cost the same in the England – 360 euros.

**Tom**   What? The wife my is crazy!

**Kate**   But this the T-shirt for the golf was very cheap. Size 42, only 27 euros. Here is a newspaper in the English and now not has tennis in the TV?

32

# Pame ya psonia

🔊 CD1, tr 17

Tom and Kate have rented a holiday apartment for a week near Athens. Kate plans to do some shopping, but Tom has other ideas...

**Kate**  Simera prepi na kanoome ta psonia. Pame sto kendro me to leoforio.

**Tom**  Ala o keros ine kakos, kani krio ke exi poli spor stin tileorasi – to golf stis thio ke misi.

**Kate**  Lipame, ala prepi na pame prota stin mixani analipsis ke sto taxithromio i sto periptero ya gramatosima... meta sto farmakio ke sto stegnokaTHaristirio.

**Tom**  Etsi, oxi golf...isos to pothosfero stis teseris ke tetarto. Afto ine olo?

**Kate**  Oxi, prepi na pame se ena polikatastima na agorasoome mia kenooryia valitsa. Meta prepi na pao sto soopermarket ke sto komotirio. Ke meta THelo na agoraso papootsia.

**Tom**  THee moo! Mexri pote ine ta magazia anixta?

**Kate**  Mexri tis epta ke misi, pistevo.

**Tom**  Etsi oxi pothosfero... isos to tenis stis okto.

*(Argotera...)*

**Kate**  Ya soo Tom, etho ine ta psonia: thiakosia gramaria zambon, ena komati tiri, miso kilo mila, thio kila patates, feta, zaxari, psomi, vootiro, merika avga, eksi bires ke ena bookali krasi. Agorasa para pola pragmata.

**Tom**  Then pirazi. XTHes then fagame poli. Ke ti ine stin megali tsanda? Kati ya mena?

**Kate**  Lipon, konda sto Notos Galleries itan ena mikro magazi ke itha kati papootsia poo itan sto noomero moo. Then ine omorfa? Aspra ke ble. O politis itan poli kalos ke omorfos san ton Tom Cruise.

**Tom**  Pios ine o Tom Cruise? Ke poso kostisan ta papootsia?

**Kate**  Itan ligo pio akriva, ala kostizoon to ithio stin Anglia – triakosia eksinda evro.

**Tom**  Ti? I yineka moo ine treli!

**Kate**  Ala afto to bloozaki ya to golf itan poli ftino. Noomero saranda thio, mono ikosi epta evro. Etho ine mia efimeritha sta Anglika, ke tora then exi tenis stin tileorasi?

# New words

🔊 CD1, tr 18

Learn the **New words** in half the time using flash cards. There are 24 to start you off.

ta ps**o**nia *the shopping*
s**i**mera *today*
pr**e**pi na *we must*
kan**oo**me *do (we)*
k**e**ndro *centre*
leof**o**rio *bus*
ker**o**s *weather; time*
kak**o**s/ia/**o** *bad*
kani kr**i**o *it is cold (lit. it makes cold)*
i tile**o**rasi *the television*
lip**a**me *I'm sorry*
pr**o**ta *first*
mix**a**ni an**a**lipsis *cashpoint machine*
taxithr**o**mio *post office*
perg**i**ptero *kiosk (it sells stamps)*
met**a** *then, afterwards*
gramat**o**sima *stamps*
farm**a**kio *chemist's*
stegnokaTHarist**i**rio *dry cleaner's*
**e**tsi *therefore, in that case*
poth**o**sfero *football*
aft**o**s/i/**o** *this*
**o**los, **o**li, **o**lo, **o**li, **o**les, **o**la *all*
polikat**a**stima *department store*
agor**a**soome *buy (we)*
ken**oo**ryios/a/o *new*
val**i**tsa *suitcase*
to komot**i**rio *the hairdresser's*
TH**e**lo *I want*
mag**a**zi, mag**a**zia *shop, shops*
agor**a**so *buy (I)*
ta pap**oo**tsia *the shoes*

THee moo! *good grief!*
p**o**te *when?*
an**i**xta *open*
pist**e**vo *I believe/think*
arg**o**tera *later*
gram**a**ria *grams*
kom**a**ti *piece*
t**i**ri *cheese*
k**i**lo *kilo*
pat**a**tes *potatoes*
z**a**xari *sugar*
ps**o**mi *bread*
v**oo**tiro *butter*
merik**i/e**s/a *some, several*
avg**o**, avg**a** *egg, eggs*
b**i**ra, b**i**res *beer, beers*
book**a**li *bottle*
kras**i** *wine*
agor**a**sa *I bought, I have bought*
para pol**a** *too many*
pr**a**gma, pr**a**gmata *thing, things*
then pir**a**zi *it doesn't matter*
xTH**e**s *yesterday*
fag**a**me *we ate, have eaten*
ts**a**nda *bag*
men**a** *me*
lip**o**n *well...*
to N**o**tos Galleries *a well-known Greek department store*
**i**tan *was/were*
**i**tha *I saw*
n**oo**mero *size, number*
**a**spros/i/o *white*
ble *blue*
pol**i**tis *sales assistant*

san *like*
pi**os**?, pi**a**?, pi**o**? *who?, which?*
kostizoon *they cost*
to **i**thio *the same*
Angl**i**a *England*

trel**os**/i/**o** *crazy*
blooz**a**ki *T-shirt*
ftin**o** *cheap*
m**i**a efimer**i**tha *a newspaper*
sta Anglik**a** *in English*

> **TOTAL NEW WORDS: 76…**
> only 157 words to go!

## More extras

### Ta xromata – *colours*

| | |
|---|---|
| **a**spro | *white* |
| m**a**vro | *black* |
| k**o**kino | *red* |
| ble | *blue* |
| pr**a**sino | *green* |
| k**i**trino | *yellow* |
| kaf**e** | *brown* |
| gri | *grey* |
| portokal**i** | *orange* |
| roz | *pink* |

# Spot the keys

◆)) CD1, tr 19

By now you can say many things in Greek. But what happens if you ask a question and don't understand the answer – hitting you at the speed of a machine gun? The smart way is not to panic, but to listen only for the words you know. Any familiar words that you pick up will provide you with key words – clues to what the other person is saying. If you have the recording, listen to the following dialogue. If you don't – read on.

You are trying to ask the way to the post office...

**You**     Signomi, poo ine to taxithromio parakalo?

**Answer**  To taxithromio then ine etho konda. *Ya va* to *vris* prepi
            *napas* sto *telostoothromookenaproxorisisya enamiliperipoo*.
            Eki *stripse* theksia ke ine konda se ena polikatastima *san*
            to Notos Galleries. Thexia ine ena ble magazi ke *apenandi*
            ine i trapeza. Eki ine to taxithromio!

Can you find your way with the key words? I think you'll get there.

# Good news grammar

🔊 CD1, tr 20

## 1 Doing more things with verbs: the past

To talk about something that happened before or in the past in Greek, you need to change the verb. This happens in two stages: First you learn the pattern in Greek for *I did*, or *I went*, or *I could* and then you learn the pattern for the other verb endings. Remember the endings of the present tense? '-o-ete/ite', '-i', '-oome' and '-oon(e)'? For the past tense it's '-a', '-ate', '-e', '-ame' and '-an(e)'. Look at the pattern for *buy*:

| *I bought* | ag**o**ras-a | *we bought* | ag**o**ras-ame |
| *you bought* | ag**o**ras-ata | *they bought* | ag**o**ras-ane |
| *he/she/it bought* | ag**o**ras-e | | |

Spend a couple of minutes on these every day until you know them in your sleep. If all fails stick them on the fridge!

Among the 30 verbs there's one 'rebel', one that's different in the past tense. So you'd better learn it straight away:

| *I was* | *you were* | *he/she/it was* | *we were* | *they were* |
| im**oo**na | is**a**ste | **i**tan | im**a**ste | **i**tan(e) |

Here are some more everyday verbs which you'll need both in the present and in the past – now you know how it's done.

| *I have* | **e**xo | *I had* | **i**xa |
| *I do* | k**a**no | *I did* | **e**kana |
| *I go* | p**a**o | *I went* | p**i**ga |
| *I work* | thool**e**vo | *I worked* | thool**e**psa |
| *I need* | xri**a**zome | *I needed* | xri**a**stika |
| *I can* | bor**o** | *I could* | bor**e**sa |
| *I fix* | fti**a**xno | *I fixed* | eft**i**aksa |
| *I eat* | tr**o**-o | *I ate* | ef**a**ga |
| *I take* | p**e**rno | *I took* | p**i**ra |
| *I want* | TH**e**lo | *I wanted* | **i**THela |
| *I think/believe* | pist**e**vo | *I thought* | pist**e**psa |
| *I see* | vl**e**po | *I saw* | **i**tha |

That's quite a list! Take a few minutes *every day* to learn these – don't try to do it all in one go.

The ones starting with an 'e' sometimes lose it along the line ('**e**kana', but '**ka**nate'), but don't worry about it.

## 2 *na* ('to'): makes sense

Pr**e**pi na p**a**o.          *I must (to) go.*
Bor**oo**me na p**a**me.   *We can (to) go.*

So what is the **na** (*to*) doing there? Think of *must* as *have to* and of *can* as *are able to…* and it makes sense.

# Let's speak Greek

◀)) CD2, tr 1

Over to you! Cover up the answers below. Always answer out loud. Start with a ten-point warm-up. Say in Greek:

**1** Now we must go.

**2** I want to do the shopping.

**3** Are the shops open?

**4** I am sorry, but it is very expensive.

**5** Is there a bus for the centre?

**6** We ate at the Taverna Aliki.

**7** Can we buy wine at the supermarket?

**8** It costs 130 euros.

**9** We have been here from three to half past four.

**10** Good grief, the wine was expensive!

Answer in Greek using '**O**xi'. Speak about yourself.

**11** Xriazeste mia mihani analipsis?

**12** Exi pothosfero stin tileorasi?

**13** Agorasate tipota sto farmakio?

Answer in Greek using the words in brackets.

**14** Ti agorasate? (tipota = *nothing*)

**15** Pote piyenete (*go*) sto pothosfero? (simera, stis thio)

**16** Mexri pote ine anixta ta magazia? (mexri tis eksi)

**17** Pios efage para poli? (Emis, fagame)

**18** Poo ithate tin valitsa? (itha, magazi)

**19** Agorasate gramatosima etho? (oxi, sto taxithromio)

**20** Ti kero kani simera? (kani krio, simera)

## Answers

1 Tora prepi na pame.
2 THelo na kano ta psonia.
3 Ine ta magazia anixta?
4 Lipame, ala ine poli akrivo.
5 Exi leoforio ya to kendro?
6 Fagame stin taverna Aliki.
7 Boroome na agorasoome krasi sto soopermarket?
8 Kostizi ekato trianda evro.
9 Imaste etho apo tis tris mexri tis teseris ke misi.
10 THee moo, to krasi itan akrivo!
11 Oxi then xriazome mia mixani analipsis.
12 Oxi, then exi pothosfero stin tileorasi.
13 Oxi, then agorasa tipota sto farmakio.
14 Then agorasa tipota.
15 Piyeno sto pothosfero simera stis thio.
16 Ta magazia ine anixta mexri tis eksi.
17 Emis fagame para poli.
18 Itha tin valitsa se ena magazi.
19 Oxi, agorasa ta gramatosima sto taxithromio.
20 O keros ine kakos. Kani krio simera.

# Let's speak more Greek

🔊 CD2, tr 2

For these optional exercises add an extra 15 minutes to your daily schedule. And remember, don't worry about getting the article or endings wrong. Near enough is good enough!

## In your own words

This exercise will teach you to express yourself freely. Use only the words you have learned so far.

Tell me in your own words that...

1 you must go shopping today
2 you are aiming for the middle of the town
3 you want the bus
4 you have to go first to a cashpoint machine...
5 ...then you have to go to the pharmacy
6 you saw a supermarket but it was not open
7 you have to buy black shoes, size 37
8 you bought the shoes, they were a bit expensive
9 you did not buy much in the supermarket
10 you bought bread, a piece of cheese and a bottle of white wine

### Answers

1 Prepi na pao ya psonia simera.
2 THelo na pao sto kendro.
3 THelo to leoforio.
4 Prepi na pao prota se mia mixani analipsis.
5 ...meta, prepi na pao sto farmakio.
6 Itha ena soopermarket, ala then itan anixto.
7 Prepi na agoraso mavra papootsia, noomero trianda epta.
8 Agorasa ta papootsia, ala itan ligo akriva.
9 Then agorasa pola pragmata sto soopermarket.
10 Agorasa psomi, ena komati tiri ke ena bookali aspro krasi.

# Let's speak Greek – fast and fluently

🔊 CD2, tr 3

Translate each section and check if it is correct, then cover up the answers and say the three or four sentences fast!

Try to say them in 20 seconds.

Some of the English is in 'Greek-speak' to help you.

*Excuse me, are you buying a television?*
*Is it expensive, the white television?*
*No, not too much. In England costs the same.*

Signomi. Agorazete mia tileorasi?
Ine akrivi, i aspri tileorasi?
Oxi, oxi poli. Stin Anglia kostizi to ithio.

*We would like to buy a suitcase.*
*We have a suitcase but it is too small.*
*I've seen a red suitcase but it is too expensive.*

THeloome na agorasoome mia valitsa.
Exoome mia valitsa ala ine poli mikri.
Itha mia kokini valitsa ala ine poli akrivi.

*The weather was bad in April.*
*I was in Volos. I ate in the town centre.*
*The restaurant was very expensive – 300 euros.*
*The waiter wasn't handsome but he was very nice.*

O keros itan asximos ton Aprilio.
Imoona sto Volo. Efaga sto kendro.
To estiatorio itan poli akrivo – triakosia evro.
O servitoros then itan omorfos ala itan poli kalos.

# Learn by heart

🔊 CD2, tr 4

Say this dialogue in under a minute and with a lot of expression.

---

**Pame ya psonia**

**Tom**   Simera kani krio. Exi pothosfero stin tileorasi.

**Kate**   Lipame ala prepi na kanoome ta psonia. Then exoome
tipota* na fame. Prepi na pame prota stin mixani analipsis,
ke meta sto soopermarket.

*(Argotera)*

**Tom**   Etho ine ta psonia! Agorasa pola: zambon, tiri, psomi ke
gramatosima ya tin Anglia.

**Kate**   Kati ya mena? Oxi bira? Oxi krasi? Tipota ya mena? THee
moo!

*tipota: nothing

---

# Test your progress

Translate the following sentences in writing. Then check your answers and be amazed.

1  First I want to go to the cashpoint machine.
2  In this the shop the shoes cost too much.
3  Did you see my husband in the chemist's?
4  We were here until a quarter past ten.
5  We saw the tennis in England on (in) television.
6  I am sorry, but we do not have the same in red, in size (number) 44.
7  This the shop is not cheap.
8  Who repaired my telephone? You?
9  Here is the department store. But it is not open.
10  Today we did not buy too many things. Only bread and half a kilo (of) butter.
11  I ate everything – eggs, apples, potatoes and a piece (of) cheese.
12  We must do the shopping. Is this the centre?
13  Yesterday I was in the office (firm) until nine o'clock.
14  The English newspapers cost a lot in Greece.
15  Is there a bus? No? It does not matter.
16  He was a very nice sales assistant.
17  What is this? Something for me?
18  Did she buy the bag near here or at Notos Galleries?
19  Everything was very expensive. Therefore I did not buy anything.
20  We need three kilos, I believe.

Remember the **Progress chart**? You are now halfway there!

# Week 4

## Day-by-day guide

Study for 45 minutes a day – but if you are keen try 50 or 55!

### Day one

- Read **Let's go and eat**.
- Listen to/Read **Pame na fame**.
- Listen to/Read the **New words**. Learn the easy ones.

### Day two

- Repeat the dialogue. Learn the harder **New words**.
- Cut out the **Flash words** to help you.

### Day three

- Learn all the **New words** until you know them well.
- Read and learn the **Good news grammar**.

### Day four

- Listen to/Read **Learn by heart**.
- Cut out and learn the ten **Flash sentences**.

### Day five

- Read **Say it simply**.
- Listen to/Read **Let's speak Greek**.

### Day six

- Listen to/Read **Let's speak more Greek** (optional).
- Listen to/Read **Let's speak Greek – fast and fluently** (optional).
- Listen to/Read **Spot the keys**.
- Translate **Test your progress**.

### Day seven

**Are you keeping your scores above 60%? In that case... have a good day off!**

# Let's go and eat

Tom and Kate are off to dinner with an important client. Will Kate be able to handle the infamous Edith?

No more 'Greek-speak!' As you'll have realized by now not everything can be translated word for word from one language to the other. If you simply exchange the words, people may understand you and might even be amused, but saying things the Greek way will sound much better and will impress the locals.

**Kate**    Tom, someone has telephoned. He did not say why. Mr Thiamandis from Thesaloniki. Here is the number.

**Tom**    Ah yes, Pavlos Thiamandis, a good client. His firm is in Thessaloniki. I know him well. He is very nice. I have an appointment with him on Thursday. It is important.

**Tom**    *(Telephones)* Hello! Good morning Mr Thiamandis. I am Tom Walker… Yes, thank you… yes, sure, it is possible… of course… next week, very interesting… no, we have time. Wonderful! No, only two days… ah yes… when? Tonight, at eight … upstairs, by the exit… in front of the door. All right! In that case, until tonight, thank you very much, goodbye.

**Kate**    What are we doing tonight?

**Tom**    We are eating with Mr Thiamandis. In the centre, behind the church. He says that it is a new and very good restaurant. Mr Thiamandis is for three days in Athens with Edith and Peter Palmer from our company.

**Kate**    I know Edith Palmer. She is boring and thinks that she knows everything. She has a terrible dog. Well… I believe I am sick. I have a bad cold and pain. I need a doctor.

**Tom**    No, please! It's not possible! Mr Thiamandis is very important.

# Pame na fame

🔊 CD2, tr 5

Tom and Kate are off to dinner with an important client. Will Kate be able to handle infamous Edith?

**Kate**  Tom, kapios tilefonise. Then ipe yati. O kirios Thiamandis apo tin THesaloniki. Etho ine to noomero.

**Tom**  Ah, ne, o Pavlos Thiamandis, enas kalos pelatis. I eteria too ine stin THesaloniki. Ton ksero kala. Ine poli kalos. Exo ena randevoo mazi too tin Pempti. Ine simandiko.

**Tom**  *(Tilefoni)* Parakalo! Kalimera, kirie Thiamandi. Ime o Tom Walker... Ne, efxaristo... ne, vevea, ine thinaton... fisika... tin epomeni evthomatha, poli enthiaferon...oxi, exoome kero. Eksoxa! Oxi, mono thio meres... ah ne... pote? Apopse, stis okto... epano, thipla stin eksotho... brosta stin porta. Endaksi! Etsi, apopse, efxaristo poli, adio.

**Kate**  Ti kanoome apopse?

**Tom**  Trome me ton kirio Thiamandi. Sto kendro, piso apo tin eklisia. Lei oti ine kenooryio ke ena poli kalo estiatorio. O kirios Thiamandis ine ya tris meres stin ATHina me tin Edith ke ton Peter Palmer apo tin eteria mas.

**Kate**  Ksero tin Edith Palmer. Ine vareti ke pistevi oti ta kseri ola. Exi enan apesio skilo. Lipon... pistevo oti ime arosti. Exo ena kako krioma ke pono. Xriazome enan yatro.

**Tom**  Oxi, se parakalo! Then ine thinaton! O kirios Thiamandis ine poli simandikos.

*(At the restaurant...) Anthreas, the head waiter, explains the menu.*

**Anthreas**  The fish is not on the menu and for dessert today there is baklavas or ice cream.

**Pavlos**  Mrs Walker, can I help you? Perhaps a suvlaki and afterwards a salad?

**Kate**  A steak with salad, please.

**Edith**  A steak, Kate? It is too much red meat.

**Pavlos**  And you, Mr Walker, what would you like? And what do you want to drink?

**Tom**  A large suvlaki with chips and vegetables and a beer, please.

**Edith**  The vegetables have a lot of oil, Tom.

**Pavlos**  And you, Mrs Palmer?

**Edith**  I want a little grilled chicken and a glass of water, please.

*(Later...)*

**Pavlos**  Do we want fruit, or perhaps something better – the baklava? No? Nothing? Have we finished? A coffee for someone? Nobody? Well… It is late. The bill, please.

**Edith**  Mr Thiamandis, can you help me please?
How do they say 'doggy bag' in Greek?
I want a little meat for my dog.

**Kate**  But Edith, the dog is in England!

*(Sto estiatorio...) Anthreas, the head waiter, explains the menu.*

**Anthreas**  To psari then ine sto menoo ke ya epithorpio exoome simera baklava i pagoto.

**Pavlos**  Kiria Walker, boro na sas voiTHiso? Isos ena soovlaki ke meta mia salata?

**Kate**  Mia brizola me salata, parakalo.

**Edith**  Brizola, Kate? Para poli kokino kreas.

**Pavlos**  Ke esis, kirie Walker, ti THelete? Ke ti THelete na pyite?

**Tom**  Ena megalo soovlaki me patates tiganites ke laxanika ke mia bira, parakalo.

**Edith**  Ta laxanika exoone poli lathi, Tom.

**Pavlos**  Ke esis, kiria Palmer?

**Edith**  THelo kotopoolo psito ke ena potiri nero, parakalo.

*(Argotera...)*

**Pavlos**  THeloome froota, i isos kati kalitero – baklava? Oxi? Tipota? Teliosame? Kafe ya kapion? Kanis? Lipon... ine arga. Ton logariasmo, parakalo.

**Edith**  Kirie Thiamandi, borite na me voiTHisete, parakalo? Pos lene 'doggy bag' sta Elinika? THelo ligo kreas ya ton skilo moo.

**Kate**  Ma Edith, o skilos ine stin Anglia!

# New words

🔊 CD2, tr 6

kapios, kapion *someone*
tilefonise *(has) telephoned*
ipe *he/she/it said*
yati *why*
pelatis *client*
ksero *I know*
kala *well*
randevoo *appointment*
mazi too *with him*
Pempti *Thursday*
simandiko *important*
parakalo *not at all (and what you
    say when answering the phone)*
efxaristo/efxaristo poli *thank
    you/thank you very much*
thinaton *possible*
fisika *of course/naturally*
tin epomeni evthomatha *next week*
enthiaferon, enthiaferoossa
    *interesting*
kero *time*
eksoxa *wonderful*
apopse *tonight*
epano *up/upstairs*
thipla *by, next to*
eksothos *exit*
brosta *in front of*
porta *door*
endaksi *all right, OK*
trome *we eat*
piso apo *behind*
eklisia *church*
lei *he/she says*
oti *that*
estiatorio *restaurant*
mas *our*

pistevi *he/she/it believes*
kseri *he/she/it knows*
apesio *terrible*
skilos *dog*
arostos/i *sick*
krioma *cold/flu*
pono *pain*
yatros *doctor*
psari *fish*
menoo *menu*
epithorpio *dessert*
baklavas *famous Greek pastry*
pagoto *ice cream*
voiTHiso *to help*
soovlaki *Greek meat dish
    (like shish kebab)*
salata *salad*
kreas *meat*
brizola *steak*
(na) pyite *to drink*
patates tiganites *chips*
laxanika *vegetables*
lathi *oil*
kotopoolo *chicken*
psito *grilled*
potiri *glass*
nero *water*
froota *fruit*
teliosame *we've finished/we
    finished*
kanis *nobody/anyone*
arga *late; slow(ly)*
borite na me voiTHisete *can you
    help me?*
Pos lene sta Elinika … *How do you
    say in Greek …?*

TOTAL NEW WORDS: 65
…only 92 words to go!

## Last easy extras

### Meres tis evthomathas – *Days of the week*

| | | | |
|---|---|---|---|
| Theftera | *Monday* | Paraskevi | *Friday* |
| Triti | *Tuesday* | Savato | *Saturday* |
| Tetarti | *Wednesday* | Kiriaki | *Sunday* |
| Pempti | *Thursday* | | |

# Good news grammar

🔊 CD2, tr 7

## 1 Verbs again

Here are the new verbs that appeared in the dialogue in Week 4.
Once again I'll give you both the present and the past as the base
for your mental acrobatics.

| | | | |
|---|---|---|---|
| *I say* | leo* | *I said* | **i**pa |
| *I know* | ks**e**ro | *I knew* | **i**ksera |
| *I help* | voiTH**o** | *I helped* | voiTH**i**sa |
| *I phone* | tilef**o**no | *I phoned* | tilef**o**nisa |

*'Leo' is a rebel (see Week 6, **Good news grammar**)

Four pairs – eight minutes to learn. And then you can say a whole
lot more, such as – what you said, whom you phoned, and what
you knew… Go for it!

And more good news, if you ever get confused or forget: there's a
complete summary of verbs in Week 6 **Good news grammar**. Have
a sneak preview. You'll know most of these in three weeks' time.

And if all else fails you can always say 'Pos l**e**ne sta Elinik**a**…?' And
everyone will be rushing to help.

## 2 'It', 'her', 'him' and 'them'

Imagine you're talking about certain things – wine, the company,
holidays or seats on the plane, or certain people – Tom, Kate, a client.
Now imagine you are just referring to these things, or people without
actually saying their name. You would say *it* or *them*.

In Greek *it, her, him* are 'ton, tin, to' and *them* is 'tous, tis, ta',
depending on the word you are referring to.

| | | | |
|---|---|---|---|
| agor**a**zo to krasi | → | to agor**a**zo | *(I buy it)* |
| agor**a**zo tin bira | → | tin agor**a**zo | *(I buy it)* |
| agor**a**zo ta pap**oo**tsia | → | ta agor**a**zo | *(I buy them)* |
| ks**e**ro tous yatrous | → | tous ks**e**ro | *(I know them)* |
| ks**e**ro ta spitia | → | ta ks**e**ro | *(I know them)* |

Did you notice? The *it* or *them* always goes in front of the verb;
*it I buy, it you buy, them we know.*

## 3 'Think' and 'know'

Here are two more everyday verbs which deserve some extra attention. By now you know the sequence: it's always *I – you – he/she/it – we – they*.

*know*: ksero

| now: | ksero | kserete | kseri | kseroome | kseroon(e) |
| --- | --- | --- | --- | --- | --- |
| yesterday: | iksera | kserate | iksere | kserame | kseran(e) |

*think/believe:* pistevo

| today | | last year | |
| --- | --- | --- | --- |
| pistevo | pistevoome | pistepsa | pistepsame |
| pistevete | pistevoon(e) | pistepsate | pistepsan(e) |
| pistevi | | pistepse | |

## 4 Attention!

Here's something unusual and different from other languages: when you want to say in Greek *he can go* you actually say: *he can goes* – 'bori na pai'. When the two verbs come together: *able to + go* or *want to + go*, note they both take the same ending.

Boroome na pame. THelo na pao.

## 5 Best news: *prepi na* – 'must/have to'

'Prepi na' never changes: no endings to learn! *I must*, *you must*, *we must*... It's always 'prepi na'. If you want to make sure *who must* you can add the person: 'ego, emis, esis', etc.

Good news grammar

53

# Learn by heart

🔊 CD2, tr 8

Here is a short piece about someone who is rather fed up. Put yourself in his shoes. Learn it and act it out in under 50 seconds.

A  Kserete ton kirio Andoni? Tilefonise tora. THeli na fao mazi too.

B  Yati?

A  Ine enas simandikos pelatis. Mono poo then ine kalos. Troi ke pini para poli.

B  Ke pote?

A  Apopse! Exi pothosfero stin tileorasi. THelo na po* oti ime arostos ala then boro… panda** i eteria! THee moo!

B  Aah… Lipame.

*po: *say* **panda: *always*

# Say it simply

When people want to speak Greek but don't dare, it's usually because they are trying to translate what they want to say from English into Greek. And because they don't know some of the words they give up!

With **Fast Greek with Elisabeth Smith** you work around the words you don't know with the words you do know. And believe me, 370 words are enough to say anything. It may not always be very elegant, but who cares? You are speaking and communicating.

Here are three examples, showing you how to say things in a simple way. The English words which are not part of the vocabulary are in bold.

1 You need to **change your flight** to London from Tuesday to Friday.

This is what you could say – simply:

THelo na paro to aeroplano ya to Lonthino tin Paraskevi, oxi tin Triti.

*I want to take the aeroplane for London on Friday, not on Tuesday.*

2 You want to get your **purse** and **mobile phon**e from the **coach** which the driver has locked.

Say it simply:

Signomi. Prepi na paro ta lefta moo ke to kinito moo apo to leoforio.

*Excuse me, I must take my money and mobile (phone) from the bus.*

3 This time your friend has **broken the heel** of her **only pair** of shoes. You have to **catch** a plane and need some help now.

This is what you could say:

Signomi, ta papootsia tis filis moo then ine endaksi.

*Excuse me, the shoe, my heel, it is not OK.*

Prepi na ta ftiaksoome ke na pame sto aeroplano. Xriazome voiTHia tora.

*I might fix them and go to the aeroplane. I need help now.*

# Let's speak Greek

🔊 CD2, tr 9

Here are eight sentences to say in Greek, and then on to greater things.

1 I am sorry, I do not have time.
2 Are we going with him?
3 I want (would like) a salad.
4 We were here yesterday.
5 Excuse me, what did you say?
6 I did not take it.
7 When did you work in Greece?
8 We did not do anything.

Now pretend you are in Greece with English friends who do not speak Greek. They will want you to ask someone something and will want you to do it for them in Greek. They will say: *Please ask him...* Start with 'Sign**o**mi...

9 if he knows Mr Thiamandis.
10 where he bought the stamps.
11 if he has an appointment now.
12 where the restaurant is.

Now your friends will ask you to tell someone something. They use some words which you don't know, so you have to work and it using words you do. Your friends will say: *Please tell her that...* Start your sentence with 'Lip**a**me...'

13 her soovlaki is cold.
14 we are having only water, no wine.
15 she is a vegetarian.
16 he does not have the number.

While shopping you are offered various items. You take them all, saying *yes, I take it* using the right form of *it*.

17 ta fr**oo**ta?
18 to pagot**o**?
19 tin b**i**ra?
20 ton kaf**e**?

## Answers

1 Lipame, then exo kero/xrono.
2 Pame mazi too?
3 THelo mia salata.
4 Imaste etho xTHes.
5 Signomi, ti ipate?
6 Then to pira.
7 Pote thoolepsate stin Elatha?
8 Then kaname tipota.
9 Signomi, kserete ton kirio Thiamandi?
10 Signomi, poo agorasate ta gramatosima?
11 Signomi, exete ena randevoo tora?
12 Signomi, poo ine to estiatorio?
13 Lipame, to soovlaki tis ine krio.
14 Lipame, exoome mono nero, oxi krasi.
15 Lipame, then troi kreas.
16 Lipame, then exi to noomero.
17 Ne, ta perno.
18 Ne, to perno.
19 Ne, tin perno.
20 Ne, ton perno.

# Let's speak more Greek

🔊 CD2, tr 10

## In your own words

This exercise will teach you to express yourself freely. Use only the words you have learned so far.

Tell me in your own words that...

1 somebody telephoned – it was Pavlos
2 you have an appointment with him next week
3 he works for a firm in Athens
4 he is a good client
5 you're going to eat in a new restaurant
6 you've got a bad cold – you need a doctor
7 you don't have time to go to the doctor
8 you can go to the chemist
9 you'd like a steak with potatoes and salad
10 you went home at half past eleven

## Answers

1 Kapios tilefonise – itan o Pavlos.
2 Exo randevoo mazi too tin epomeni evthomatha.
3 Thoolevi ya mia eteria stin ATHina.
4 Ine kalos pelatis.
5 Trome se ena kenoorio estiatorio.
6 Exo ena asximo krioma – xriazome enan yatro.
7 Then exo kero na pao sto yatro.
8 Boro na pao sto farmakio.
9 THelo mia brizola me patates ke mia salata.
10 Piga sto spiti stis entheka ke misi.

# Let's speak Greek – fast and fluently

🔊 CD2, tr 11

Translate each section and check if it is correct, then cover up the answers and say the three or four sentences fast!

Try to say them in 20 seconds.
Some of the English is in 'Greek-speak' to help you.

*Do you know Ari Thiamandis? He phoned yesterday.*
*Why? He said it was important.*
*The appointment in Athens was on Wednesday.*

Kserete ton **A**ri Thiamand**i**? Tilef**o**nise xTHes.
Yat**i**? **I**pe **o**ti **i**tan simandik**o**.
To randev**oo** stin Athina **i**tan tin Tet**a**rti.

*Ari is in Athens for three days.*
*There is a restaurant behind the church.*
*Ari says it's very good.*

O **A**ris ine stin Ath**i**na ya tris m**e**res.
**E**xi **e**na estiat**o**rio p**i**so ap**o** tin eklis**i**a.
O **A**ris l**e**i **o**ti ine pol**i** kal**o**.

*Unfortunately, I can't go to the restaurant.*
*My dog is ill. He has eaten too much meat.*
*Oh, I am very sorry. How do you say in Greek: 'Poor little thing?'*
**(o kaimenos)**

Thistix**o**s, then bor**o** na p**a**o sto estiat**o**rio.
O sk**i**los moo ine ar**o**stos. **E**faye p**a**ra pol**i** kr**e**as.
O, lip**a**me pol**i**. Pos l**e**ne sta Elinik**a**: 'Poor little thing'? O kaim**e**nos.

Now say all the sentences in Greek without stopping and starting.

# Spot the keys

🔊 CD2, tr 12

You practised listening for key words when you asked the way to the post office in Week 3. Now you are in a department store. You have asked the sales assistant if the black dress you liked is also available in size 44. She said: '**O**xi, m**i**a stigm**i**, parakal**o**...' and disappeared. When she came back this is what she said:

*Thistix*Os **ex**oome n**oo**mero saranda t**e**sera m**o**no se pr**a**sino. *Then exoome kanena mavro forema se afto to meye THos.* Al**a** **ex**oome *mavra foremata* se n**oo**mero saranda thio *yali poli pelates zitoone afto* to *meye THos.* To n**oo**mero saranda thio *mavro pistevo*, **i**ne ark**e**ta megalo *ya sas.*

It appears that size 44 was only available in green but she believes that size 42 might be big enough.

# Test your progress

Translate in writing. Then check your answers.

1 Has someone telephoned Mr Thiamandis?

2 I want to know where the restaurant is.

3 It is late and he is not there. What are we doing tonight?

4 Here is the menu! Do you know the wines of Ahaia?

5 The cashpoint machine is upstairs, behind the exit, near the door.

6 Wednesday we must go to the doctor. It is an important appointment.

7 Why do I say she is boring? Because I know her well.

8 Did you see him? I must go to Larisa with him.

9 Mr Thiamandis is my client. He has bought everything.

10 I want to buy this thing. How does one say in Greek…?

11 Next week? I am sorry. It is not possible.

12 Can you help me please? Many thanks!

13 Three hundred euros for two days. Very interesting. Yes, of course we take it.

14 I must buy three things for my friends.

15 I have a cold. I need a doctor.

16 Can they eat only the baklava?

17 There is a terrible dog. What can we do?

18 Nobody saw who ate the steak.

19 Can I say something: the chicken is not bad but the fish is better.

20 What do you take? The fruit? Yes, sure, it is from Ahaia.

If you are happy with your result take it straight to the **Progress Chart**.

# Week 5

## Day-by-day guide

How about 15 minutes on the train, tube or bus, 10 minutes on the way home and 20 minutes before switching on the television…?

### Day one

- Read **On the move**.
- Listen to/Read **Taksithevondas**.
- Listen to/Read the **New words**. Learn 15 or more.

### Day two

- Repeat the dialogue. Learn the harder **New words**.
- Cut out the **Flash words** to get stuck in.

### Day three

- Test yourself to perfection on all the **New words**.
- Read and learn the **Good news grammar**.

### Day four (the tough day)

- Listen to/Read **Learn by heart**.
- Cut out and learn the ten **Flash sentences**.

### Day five

- Listen to/Read **Let's speak Greek**.
- Go over **Learn by heart**.

### Day six

- Listen to/Read **Let's speak more Greek** (optional).
- Listen to/Read **Let's speak Greek – fast and fluently** (optional).
- Listen to/Read **Spot the keys**.
- Translate **Test your progress**.

### Day seven

**I bet you don't want a day off… but I insist!**

# On the move

Tom and Kate travel through Southern Greece – by train, bus and hire car.

*(At the station...)*

**Tom**  Two tickets for Patras, please.

**Clerk**  Withreturn?

**Tom**  With what? Can you speak more slowly, please?

**Clerk**  With–return?

**Tom**  No, one way only. What time is there a train and from which platform?

**Clerk**  At ten minutes to four. Platform eight.

**Kate**  Quickly, Tom, here are two seats, non-smoking. Oh, but someone is smoking. Excuse me, you cannot smoke, because it is non-smoking here. It is forbidden to smoke.

**Man**  I am sorry. I don't understand, I speak only English.

*(At the bus stop...)*

**Kate**  There is no bus. We have to wait 20 minutes. Tom, here are my postcards. Over there is a letter box. I want to take some photos. The town is beautiful in the sun.

**Tom**  Kate, come on! There are a lot of people. Here are two buses! Both are blue. This one is full. Let's take the other one. *(On the bus...)* Two for Sparti, please.

**Driver**  This bus goes only to Corinth.

**Tom**  But we are in Corinth!

**Driver**  Yes, yes, but this is the bus for the hospital of Corinth.

# Taksithevondas

🔊 CD2, tr 13

Tom and Kate travel through Southern Greece – by train, bus and hire car.

*(Ston stathmo...)*

**Tom**  Thio isitiria ya tin Patra, parakalo.

**Clerk**  Me-epistrofi?

**Tom**  Me ti? Borite na milisete pio arga, parakalo?

**Clerk**  Me epistrofi?

**Tom**  Oxi, mono mias katefTHinsis. Ti ora exi treno ke apo pia platforma?

**Clerk**  Stis tesseris para theka. Platforma okto.

**Kate**  Grigora Tom, etho ine thio THesis, ya mi kapnizondes. Ah, ala kapios kapnizi. Signomi, then borite na kapnisete, ine ya mi kapnizondes etho. Apagorevete to kapnisma.

**Man**  Sorry, I don't understand, milao only Anglika.

*(Stin stasi leoforiou...)*

**Kate**  Then exi leoforio. Prepi na perimenoome ikosi lepta. Tom, etho ine ta kart-postal moo. Eki pera ine ena gramatokivotio. THelo na paro merikes fotografies. I poli ine poli omorfi ston ilio.

**Tom**  Kate, ela! Exi poli kosmo. Etho ine thio leoforia! Ke ta thio ine ble. Afto ine yemato. As paroome to alo.*(Sto leoforio...)* Thio ya Sparti, parakalo.

**Driver**  Afto to leoforio pai mono stin KorinTHo.

**Tom**  Ala imaste stin KorinTHo!

**Driver**  Ne, ne, ala afto ine to leoforio ya to nosokomio tis KorintTHoo.

*(In the car...)*

**Tom**      Here is our car. Only 120 euros for three days. I am very satisfied.

**Kate**     I do not like the car. It costs so little because it's very old. Let's hope that we don't have problems.

**Tom**      I am sorry. The first car was too expensive and the second (one) too big. This was the last one. *(Later...)* Where are we? There is no map! On the left there is a petrol station, and on the right there is a school. Hurry up!

**Kate**     We are coming from the underground station. The main road is at the (traffic) lights. It's perhaps three kilometres until the motorway. *(On the motorway...)* Why does the car go slowly? Have we enough petrol? How many litres? Do we have oil? Is the engine too hot? They gave us a wreck. Where is the mobile phone? Where is the number of the garage? Where is my bag?

**Tom**      Kate, please! I have a headache. And now it's raining! And why are the police behind us?

*(Sto aftokinito...)*

**Tom**  Etho ine to aftokinito mas. Mono ekatoikosi evro ya tris meres. Ime poli ikanopioimenos.

**Kate**  Then moo aresi to aftokinito. Kostizi toso ligo yati ine poli palio. As elpisoome oti then THa exoome kanena provlima.

**Tom**  Lipame. To proto aftokinito itan poli akrivo ke to theftero poli megalo. Afto itan to telefteo. *(Argotera...)* Poo imaste? Then exi xarti! Aristera ine ena venzinathiko ke theksia ine ena skolio. Kane grigora!

**Kate**  Erxomaste apo ton ipoyio. O kendrikos thromos ine sta fanaria. Ine isos tria xiliometra mexri ton aftokinitothromo. *(Ston aftokinitothromo...)* Yati pai to aftokinito arga? Exoome arketi venzini? Posa litra? Exoome lathi? Ine i mixani poli zesti? Mas ethosan ena saravalo. Poo ine to kinito tilefono? Poo ine to noomero too garaz? Poo ine i tsanda moo?

**Tom**  Kate, se parakalo! Exo ponokefalo. Ke tora vrexi! Ke yati ine i astinomia piso mas?

# New words

🔊 CD2, tr 14

taksithevondas *on the move/ travelling*
staTHmos *(railway) station*
isitirio *ticket*
me epistrofi *(with) return*
mias katefTHinsis *one way*
borite na milisete …? *can you speak …?*
pio *more*
treno *train*
pios, pia, pio *who, which*
platforma *platform*
grigora *quickly*
mi kapnizondes *non-smoking*
kapnizi *he/she/it smokes*
apagorevete to kapnisma *it's forbidden to smoke*
then katalaveno *I don't understand*
milao *I speak*
stasi *(bus) stop*
perimeno *I wait*
kart-postal *postcard*
eki pera *over there*
gramatokivotio *letter box*
fotografia *photograph*
poli *city/town*
ilios *the sun*
exi kosmo *it's crowded*
ke ta thio *both (and the two)*
yematos/i/o *full*
alo *other*
nosokomio *hospital*
aftokinito *car*
mera, meres *day, days*

ikanopioimenos/i/o *satisfied, happy*
moo aresi/then moo aresi *I like/ I don't like*
palios/ia/io *old (things)*
as elpisume *let's hope*
then THa exoome *we won't have*
provlima *problem*
proto *first*
theftero *second*
telefteo *last*
xartis, xarti *map*
venzinathiko *petrol station*
skolio *school*
kane grigora! *hurry up!*
erxomaste *we come/we're coming*
ipoyio *underground*
kendrikos thromos *main road (central road)*
fanaria *lights (also used for traffic lights)*
xiliometro *kilometre*
aftokinitothromos *motorway*
venzini *petrol*
posi, poses, posa *how many*
litro *litre*
mixani *machine/engine*
zesti *hot*
saravalo *wreck*
garaz *garage (car mechanic's garage)*
tsanda *bag*
ponokefalo *headache*
vroxi *rain (vrexi – it's raining)*
astinomia *police*

**TOTAL NEW WORDS: 59**
**…only 33 words to go!**

# Learn by heart

🔊 CD2, tr 15

Someone has bumped into the car and someone else is getting suspicious! Try to say these lines fluently and like a prize-winning play.

**Pame ya tenis**

**A**   Pame ya tenis.
Moo aresoon i thio Amerikani.
Exo isitiria apo tin eteria moo.
As paroome to leoforio i kalitera pame me ton ipoyio.
Exi treno oli tin imera.

**B**   Me to leoforio? Ton ipoyio? To treno? Yati?
Ti simveni?*
Exoome ena aftokinito eki kato.

**A**   Eh… xTHes, me tin vroxi then itha ta fanaria. Then ine tipota, mono i porta ke o mixanikos sto garaz itan poli kalos!

***Ti simveni?:** What's the matter?

# Good news grammar

🔊 CD2, tr 16

## 1 moo, sas, too, tis… (e)mena, (e)sena, afton, aftin

Learning these cold is difficult, but when they come up in the text or the **Flash cards** it's not so bad. Here's the first group:

| moo | sas | too | tis | mas | tus |
|-----|-----|-----|-----|-----|-----|
| *my* | *your* | *his* | *her* | *our* | *their* |

The second group gives you some useful combinations. Spend five minutes learning them and take another five minutes to remember.

| ya mena | ya sas (sena) | ya afton | ya aftin | ya mas | ya aftoos |
|---------|---------------|----------|----------|--------|-----------|
| *for me* | *for you* | *for him* | *for her* | *for us* | *for them* |

You use the same words with 'apo' (*from*) and 'mazi me' (*with*).

## 2 Last handful of verbs

Week 5 verbs – neatly lined up for easy learning. Ten minutes will do it.

| *I speak* | milao | *I spoke* | milisa |
|-----------|-------|-----------|--------|
| *I smoke* | kapnizo | *I smoked* | kapnisa |
| *I wait* | perimeno | *I waited* | perimena |
| *I like* | moo aresi/moo aresoon(e) | *I liked* | moo arese/ aresan |
| *I give* | thino | *I gave* | ethosa |

## 3 Last useful verb... *erxome* ('come')

'**Erxome**' is a rebel! Spend five minutes learning it while you're waiting for the bus.

|        | *I*     | *you*     | *he/she/it* | *we*       | *they*     |
|--------|---------|-----------|-------------|------------|------------|
| t**o**ra: | **e**rxome | erx**o**saste | **e**rxete | erx**o**maste | **e**rxode |
| xthes: | **i**rTHa | **i**rTHate | **i**rTHe | **i**rTHame | **i**rTHan(e) |

## 4 *Moo aresi/then moo aresi* ('I like/I don't like')

You will use this all the time. Think how often you use *I like – I don't like* in English! Unfortunately it needs a bit of mental acrobatics, because in *Greek* *I like* is literally *it pleases me*: 'moo *(me)* ar**e**si *(it pleases)*'. *I don't like* is: 'then moo ar**e**si', 'then moo ar**e**si to Internet' (*I don't like the internet*).

If several things please you it's 'moo ar**e**soon'. Example: *I like the children* – 'moo ar**e**soon ta peth**i**a'. And if *you, he* or *she*, *we* or *they* like something it would be: 'sas ar**e**si', 'too' or 'tis ar**e**si', 'mas ar**e**si' or 'toos ar**e**si'. So you have to rethink it quickly until it's as automatic as changing gear. Then: 'sas ar**e**si o Tom Cruise? – Ne, ne!'

# Let's speak Greek

🔊 CD2, tr 17

A ten-point warm-up: I give you an answer and you ask me a question as if you did not hear the words in capital letters very well.

*Example*: O Nikos ine STO TAXITHROMIO. Poo ine o Nikos?

1 Ena tilefono ya TIN EIENI SOFIANOO.
2 Imoona sto nosokomio TON MARTIO.
3 O Tom THeli na milisi ME TON KIRIO THIAMANDI.
4 To isitirio me epistrofi ya tin ATHina kostizi EKSINDATRIA EVRO.
5 Then exume kero ya ta FANARIA!
6 NE, ime ikanopioimenos me to spiti.
7 APAGOREVETE to kapnisma etho.
8 Pao stin Anglia ME TI FERRARI MOO.
9 Then ime ikanopioimenos me to spiti yati EXi POLA PROVLIMATA.
10 I thiakopes moo itan POLI KALES.

Answer in Greek using *yes* or *no*. Speak about yourself.

11 Exete venzini?
12 Erxete to treno?
13 Piyenete ston staTHmo?
14 Piyenete stin Larisa?
15 Kapnizete poli?

Explain these words in Greek. Your answers can vary from mine.

16 an au pair
17 kennel
18 a teacher
19 unemployed
20 to be broke

## Answers

1 Ya pion ine to tilefono?

2 Pote minate sto nosokomio?

3 Se pion THeli na milisi o Tom?

4 Poso kostizi to isitirio me epistrofi ya tin ATHina?

5 Exoome kero ya ta fanaria?

6 Ise ikanopioimenos me to spiti?

7 Yati then boroome na kapnisoome.

8 Pos pate stin Anglia?

9 Yati then iste ikanopioimenos me to spiti?

10 Pos itan i thiakopes soo?

11 Ne, exo venzini.

12 Oxi, then erxete to treno.

13 Oxi, then piyeno ston staTHmo.

14 Ne, piyeno stin Larisa.

15 Oxi, then kapnizo poli.

16 Kapia poo voithai sto spiti.

17 Mikro spiti ya skiloos.

18 Kapios poo thoolevi sto skolio.

19 Kapios poo then exi thoolia.

20 Otan then exete lefta.

# Let's speak more Greek

🔊 CD2, tr 18

## In your own words

This exercise will teach you to express yourself freely. Use only the words you have learned so far. Tell me in your own words that...

1 you bought a return ticket to Thessaloniki
2 there is a train at 10.15 from platform eight
3 it is not allowed, but somebody is smoking
4 on Monday you would like to go to Corinth (Korinthos) by bus
5 you must take some photos for your children
6 this bus is full; suggest that you take the other one
7 your car is cheap because it is very old
8 it is only 80 euros for four days
9 the car goes so slowly and the engine overheats
10 hopefully you won't have problems

## Answers

1 Agorasa ena isitirio ya tin THesaloniki me epistrofi.
2 Exi ena treno stis theka ke tetarto apo tin platforma okto.
3 Apagorevete, ala kapios kapnizi.
4 Tin theftera THelo na pao stin KorinTHo me to leoforio.
5 Prepi na paro merikes fotografies ya ta pethia.
6 Afto to leoforio ine yemato. As paroome to alo.
7 To aftokinito moo ine ftino yati ine poli palio.
8 Ine mono ogthonda evro ya teseris meres.
9 To aftokinito pai toso arga, ke i mixani ine poli zesti.
10 Elpizo oti then THa exo/exoome kanena provlima.

# Let's speak Greek – fast and fluently

🔊 CD2, tr 19

Translate each section and check if it is correct, then cover up the answers and say the three or four sentences fast!

Try to say them in 25 seconds.
Some of the English is in 'Greek-speak' to help you.

*A ticket to Piraeus, please, only one way.*
*How much? €21? Can you speak more slowly, please?*
*Thank you. What time is the train?*

Ena isitirio ya ton Pirea, parakalo, mono aplo.
Poso? Ikosiena evro? Borite na milisete pio arga, parakalo?
Efxaristo. Ti ora ine to treno?

*We would like to take the bus.*
*We have to wait 15 minutes.*
*We can take a photo.*

THeloome na paroome to leoforio.
Prepi na perimenoome thekapende lepta.
Boroome na paroome mia fotografia.

*We don't have a map of Greece (Elatha).*
*It's ten kilometres to the motorway.*
*The traffic lights are red.*
*We have a problem. Perhaps the car is broken (xalasmeno).*
*My wife has a headache.*

Then exoome ena xarti tis Elathos.
Ine theka xiliometra mexri ton aftokinitothromo.
Ta fanaria ine kokina.
Exoome ena provlima. Isos to aftokinito ine xalasmeno.
I yineka moo exi ponokefalo.

Now say all the sentences in Greek without stopping and starting.

Try and do it in under 90 seconds. If you're not happy with your result, try it once more.

# Spot the keys

🔊 CD2, tr 20

This time you plan a trip in the country and wonder about the weather.

**You**    Signomi, kserete ti kero kani avrio?

**Answer** Lipame, then ksero *ti kero kani* apo tin tileorasi *ala thiavasa stin efimeritha* oti o keros *THa ine astatos*. Apopse tha kani krio ke vroxi. *I THermocrasia* ine thekapende *vaTHmi* Kelsiou *ke tha exi THinato anemo*.

He doesn't know … something on television then you heard the word weather and that it's going to be cold tonight and rainy. There's also something about 15 degrees Celsius, so you'd better take a jacket and an umbrella.

# Test your progress

Translate in writing. Then check your answers and be amazed.

1 It is forbidden to go to the restaurant without shoes.
2 I like your Porsche. Was it very cheap?
3 When I am on holiday I always speak a lot of Greek.
4 I need six tickets. Do you have non-smoking seats?
5 I think that we have problems with the engine.
6 I do not like the Internet. It's very difficult.
7 I do not understand. Can you speak more slowly, please?
8 It's hot and it's crowded. Let's go to the town.
9 One hour with her gives me a headache.
10 There is a bus at the traffic lights. Where's it going?
11 The credit card isn't here. We have to telephone the police.
12 Let's do it like this: first we buy the Ferrari for me and afterwards the T-shirt for you.
13 I like this car, but the other (one) was better.
14 We have only one litre of petrol and there isn't (hasn't) a petrol station until Athens.
15 I like the sun and I like the rain. I like both.
16 (On the phone) Hello, we're 20 km from Athens. Is (has) there any garage?
17 Excuse me. I need help, please. I do not know Athens. Where is the station?
18 The main road? It's not too difficult. You take the metro.
19 Where are they? What did they do? I do not like to wait.
20 We are coming from (the) platform 17? Where is Spiros?

# Week 6

## Day-by-day guide

This is your last week! Need I say more?

### Day one

- Read **At the airport**.
- Listen to/Read **Sto aerothromio**.
- Listen to/Read the **New words**. There are only a handful.

### Day two

- Read **Sto aerothromio**. Learn all the **New words**.
- Work with the **Flash words** and **Flash sentences**.

### Day three

- Test yourself on the **Flash sentences**.
- Listen to/Read **Learn by heart**.

### Day four

- No more **Good news grammar**! Have a look at the summary.
- Read **Say it simply**.

### Day five

- Listen to/Read **Let's speak Greek**.
- Listen to/Read **Spot the keys**.

### Day six

- Listen to/Read **Let's speak more Greek** (optional).
- Listen to/Read **Let's speak Greek – fast and fluently** (optional).
- Your last **Test your progress!** Go for it.

### Day seven

```
Congratulations!
You have successfully completed the course
and can now speak
Fast Greek with Elisabeth Smith
```

# At the airport

Tom and Kate are on their way home to Birmingham. They are in the departure lounge at Athens airport.

**Tom** On Monday we must work. Terrible! I would prefer to go to Miami or Honolulu. Nobody knows where I am and the office can wait.

**Kate** And *my* company? What do they do? They speak with my mother! She has the number of my mobile. And then?

**Tom** Yes, yes, I know (it). Well, perhaps at Christmas we can go for a week in the snow or to Madeira on a ship… There is a kiosk down there. I'll go and buy a newspaper… Kate! There is Aristotelis Nikou!

**Ari** Hello, how are you? What are you doing here? This is my wife, Nancy. Are the holidays over? How were they?

**Kate** Greece is wonderful. We saw a lot and ate too much. We know Ahaia and Skiathos very well now.

**Ari** Next year Thessaloniki! What a fantastic city!… Mrs Walker, my wife would like to buy a book about computers. Can you go with her to help her, please. Mr Walker, you have a newspaper. Are there any photos of the football? And afterwards are we going to drink something?

*(At the kiosk…)*

**Kate** There is nothing here. I do not see anything interesting. Are you also going to England?

**Nancy** No, we are going to Sparti to Ari's mother. Our children are often with her in the holidays. Tomorrow we'll take the train. It costs less.

**Kate** Your husband works at the Bank of Greece?

**Nancy** Yes. The work is interesting, but the money is little. We have an apartment, but it is small, and an old car. You always need a lot of work. My family lives in California and my girlfriend is in Florida and we write a lot of letters. I would like to go to America but it is too expensive.

**Kate** But you have a beautiful house in Porto Rafti.

**Nancy** A house in Porto Rafti? I was never in Porto Rafti. When we have holidays we go to a friend in Pireus.

**Tom** Kate, come quickly! We must go. Goodbye! What is the matter, Kate?

**80** **Kate** Wait, Tom, wait…!

# Sto aerothromio

◀ CD2, tr 21

Tom and Kate are on their way home to Birmingham. They are in the departure lounge at Athens airport.

**Tom**  Tin Theftera prepi na thoolepsoome. Apesio! Protimo na pame sto Miami i stin Xonolooloo. Kanis then kseri poo ime ke i eteria bori na perimeni.

**Kate**  Ke i eteria moo? Ti kanoone? Milane stin mitera moo. Afti exi to noomero too kinitoo tilefonoo moo. Ke tote?

**Tom**  Ne, ne, to ksero. Lipon, isos ta Xristooyena boroome na pame ya mia evthomatha sto xioni i stin Matheira me karavi... Ine ena periptero eki kato. Pao na agoraso mia efimeritha... Kate! O Aristotelis Nikou!

**Ari**  Yasas, ti kanete? Ti kanete etho? Afti ine i yineka moo, i Nancy. I thiakopes teliosan? Pos itan?

**Kate**  I Elatha ine iperoxi. Ithame pola pragmata ke fagame para poli. Kseroome tin Axaya ke tin SkiaTHo poli kala tora.

**Ari**  Too xronoo i THesaloniki! Ti fandastiki poli!... Kiria Walker, i yineka moo Theli na agorasi ena vivlio ya komputer. Borite na pate mazi tis na tin voiTHisete, parakalo? Kirie Walker, exete mia efimeritha. Exi kamia fotografia pothosferoo? Ke meta pinoome kati?

*(Sto periptero...)*

**Kate**  Then exi tipota etho. Then vlepo tipota enthiaferon. Pate ke esis stin Anglia?

**Nancy**  Oxi, pame stin Sparti, stin mitera too Ari. Ta pethia mas ine sixna mazi tis stis thiakopes. Avrio pernoome to treno. Kostizi pio ligo.

**Kate**  O anthras sas thoolevi stin Trapeza tis Elathos?

**Nancy**  Ne. I thoolia ine enthiaferoossa ala ta lefta ine liga. Exoome ena thiamerisma, ala ine mikro, ke ena palio aftokinito. Panda xriazete poli thoolia. I ikoyenia moo meni stin Kalifornia ke i fili moo ine stin Floritha ke grafoome pola gramata. THelo na pao stin Ameriki ala ine poli akriva.

**Kate**  Ala exete ena omorfo spiti sto Porto Rafti.

**Nancy**  Ena spiti sto Porto Rafti? Then imoon pote sto Porto Rafti. Otan exoome thiakopes pame se enan filo ston Pirea.

**Tom**  Kate, ela grigora! Prepi na pame. Adio! Ti simveni, Kate?

**Kate**  Perimene, Tom, perimene...!

# New words

🔊 CD2, tr 22

aerothromio *airport*
protimo/protimisa *I prefer/
  I preferred*
bori na perimeni *it can wait*
kanoone *they do/make*
milane *they speak*
mitera *mother*
too *of*
ke tote? *and then?*
Xristooyena *Christmas*
xioni *snow*
karavi *boat*
eki kato *down there*
ti kanete? *How are you?*
teliosan *are finished*
iperoxos/i/o *wonderful*
kseroome *we know*
too xronoo *next year*

fandastikos/i/o *fantastic*
vivlio *book*
vlepo *I see*
sixna *often*
thiamerisma *apartment*
ikoyenia *family*
meni *he/she/it lives or stays*
meno/emina *I live/I lived*
grafoome *we write*
grafo/egrapsa *I write/I wrote*
gramata *letters*
pote *never/ever*
otan *when*
ela!/elate! *come! (familiar/
  formal)*
ti simveni? *what's the matter?*
perimene/perimenete *wait!
  (familiar/formal)*

> **TOTAL NEW WORDS: 33**
> **Total Greek words learned: 370**
> **Extra words: 81**
> **GRAND TOTAL: 451**

# Learn by heart

🔊 CD2, tr 23

This is your last dialogue to learn by heart. Give it your best! You now have a large store of everyday sayings which will be very useful.

---

**Adio!**

**Kate**  Parakalo. Kalimera kirie Thiamandi. Ime i Kate Walker. Imaste sto aerothromio. Ne, I thiakopes teliosan. I Elatha ine iperoxi. O Tom theli na sas milisi*. Mia stigmi parakalo, e... adio!

**Tom**  Ya, Pavlo! Ti? Agorases ke ta thio? Ine ena e-mail stin eteria moo? Iperoxa! Efxaristo poli! Too xronoo? I Kate THeli na pai stin Italia ala ego THelo na tho tin THesaloniki. Me tin Edith Palmer? SE PARAKALO! Prepi na pame, lipon, THa sas tho sindoma! Yas sas, adio!

*THeli na sas milisi: *wants to talk to you*

# Spot the keys

🔊 CD2, tr 24

Here is a final practice round. If you have the recording close the book right now. This time the key words are not shown. When you have found them see if you can get the gist of it.

This is what you might ask of a taxi driver:

| You | Posa lepta mexri to aerothromio ke poso kostizi? |
|---|---|
| Answer | *Eksartate pote pate. Kanonika perni ikosi lepta. Ala an exi poli kinisi ke exi pola aftokinita stin yefira perni toolaxiston triandapende lepta. Borite na thiavasete tin timi sto taximetro. Ine metaksi eksinda ke enthominda evro.* |

# Good news grammar

As promised there is no new grammar in this section, just a summary of all the verbs which appear in the six weeks. The second line of each entry is the past tense. The 30 verbs are not for learning, just for a quick check. You know and have used most of them!

| | I | you | he/she/it | we | they |
| | ego | esis | aftos/afti/ afto | emis | afti |
|---|---|---|---|---|---|
| **be** | ime | isaste | ine | imaste | ine |
| | *imoon* | *isaste* | *itan* | *imastan* | *itan(e)* |
| **buy** | agorazo | agorazete | agorazi | agorazoome | agorazoon(e) |
| | *agorasa* | *agorasate* | *agorase* | *agorasame* | *agorasan(e)* |
| **can** | boro | borite | bori | boroome | boroon(e) |
| | *boresa* | *boresate* | *borese* | *boresame* | *boresan(e)* |
| **come** | erxome | erxosaste | erxete | erxomaste | erxode |
| | *irTHa* | *irTHate* | *irTHe* | *irTHame* | *irTHan(e)* |
| **cost** | | | costizi | | costizoon(e) |
| | | | *costise* | | *costisan* |
| **drink** | pino | pinete | pini | pinoome | pinoon(e) |
| | *ipia* | *ipiate* | *ipie* | *ipiame* | *ipiane* |
| **do** | kano | kanete | kani | kanoome | kanoon(e) |
| | *ekana* | *kanate* | *ekane* | *kaname* | *ekanan* |
| **eat** | troo | trote | troi | trome | trone |
| | *efaga* | *fagate* | *efaye* | *(e)fagame* | *fagane* |
| **fix, repair** | ftiaxno | ftiaxnete | ftiaxni | ftiaxnoome | ftiaxnoon(e) |
| | *eftiaksa* | *ftiaksate* | *eftiakse* | *ftiaksame* | *ftiaksan(e)* |
| **give** | thino | thinete | thini | thinoome | thinoon(e) |
| | *ethosa* | *thosate* | *ethose* | *thosame* | *thosane* |
| **go** | pao | pate | pai | pame | pane |
| | *piga* | *pigate* | *piye* | *pigame* | *pigan(e)* |
| **have** | exo | exete | exi | exoome | exoon(e) |
| | *ixa* | *ixate* | *ixe* | *ixame* | *ixan(e)* |
| **help** | voiTHo | voiTHite | voiTHi | voiTHoome | voiTHoon(e) |
| | *voiTHisa* | *voiTHisate* | *voiTHises* | *voiTHisame* | *voiTHisan(e)* |
| **know** | ksero | kserete | kseri | kseroome | kseroon(e) |
| | *iksera* | *kserate* | *iksere* | *kserame* | *kserane* |
| **like** | | | aresi | | aresoon(e) |
| | | | *arese* | | *aresane* |
| **live** | meno | menete | meni | menoome | menoon(e) |
| | *emina* | *minate* | *emine* | *miname* | *minane* |
| **must** | prepi | | | | |

*(Contd)* 85

| | I | you | he/she/it | we | they |
|---|---|---|---|---|---|
| **need** | xriazome | xriazosaste | xriazete | xriazomaste | xriazode |
| | *xriastika* | *xriastikate* | *xriastike* | *xriastikame* | *xriastikan* |
| **prefer** | protimo | protimite | protimi | protimoome | protimoon(e) |
| | *protimisa* | *protimisate* | *protimise* | *protimisame* | *protimisane* |
| **say** | leo | lete | lei | leme | lene |
| | *ipa* | *ipate* | *ipe* | *ipame* | *ipane* |
| **see** | vlepo | vlepete | vlepi | vlepoome | vlepoon(e) |
| | *itha* | *ithate* | *ithe* | *ithame* | *ithan(e)* |
| **smoke** | kapnizo | kapnizete | kapnizi | kapnizoome | kapnizoon(e) |
| | *kapnisa* | *kapnisate* | *kapnise* | *kapnisame* | *kapnisan* |
| **speak** | milao | milate | milai | milame | milane |
| | *milisa* | *milisate* | *milise* | *milisame* | *milisan(e)* |
| **take** | perno | pernete | perni | pernoome | pernoon(e) |
| | *pira* | *pirate* | *pire* | *pirame* | *pirane* |
| **telephone** | **tilefono** | tilefonite | tilefoni | tilefonoome | tilefinoon(e) |
| | *tilefonisa* | *tilefonisate* | *tilefonise* | *tilefonisame* | *tilefonisan* |
| **think,** | pistevo | pistevete | pistevi | pistevoome | pistevoon(e) |
| **believe** | *pistepsa* | *pistepsate* | *pistepse* | *pistepsame* | *pistepsan(e)* |
| **wait** | perimeno | perimenete | perimeni | perimenoome | perimenoon(e) |
| | *perimena* | *perimenate* | *perimene* | *perimename* | *perimenan* |
| **want,** | THelo | THelete | THeli | THeloome | THeloon(e) |
| **would like** | *iTHela* | *THelate* | *iTHele* | *THelame* | *THelane* |
| **work** | thoolevo | thoolevete | thoolevi | thoolevoome | thoolevoon(e) |
| | *thoolepsa* | *thoolepsate* | *thoolepse* | *thoolepsame* | *thoolepsan(e)* |
| **write** | grafo | grafete | grafi | grafoome | grafoon(e) |
| | *egrapsa* | *grapsate* | *egrapse* | *grapsame* | *grapsane* |

# Say it simply

1 Imagine you are at the dry cleaner's. You want to know if the item you have brought to be cleaned can be done by the end of the day since you are leaving for Athens early tomorrow morning. You also want to explain that the stain may be red wine.

Think of what you could say in simple Greek, using the words you know. Then write it down and compare it with my suggestion in the **Answers** section.

2 You are at the airport about to catch your flight home when you realize that you have left some clothes behind in the room of your hotel. You phone the hotel to ask the housekeeper to send the things on to you.

What would you say? Formulate your telephone call and say it. Then write it down and compare it with my suggestion in the **Answers** section.

# Let's speak Greek

◀》 CD2, tr 25

Here's a five-point warm-up. **Answer** these questions using the words in brackets.

1 Agorasate to thiamerisma? (ne)
2 Kserete ti kanoone ta Xristooyena? (tipota)
3 Pote ithate ton anthra sas? (XTHes)
4 Yati piyenete stin Anglia? (ikoyenia, meni, eki)
5 Pos ine i Elatha? (iperoxi)

In your last exercise you are going to act as an interpreter again this time telling your Greek friend what others have said in English. Each time say the whole sentence out loud, translating the English words in brackets.

6 I fili moo ipe oti... (the holidays are finished)
7 O John ipe oti... (we are going to Venice next year)
8 I yineka moo THeli na kseri... (when you go to Los Angeles)
9 Episis THeli na kseri... (what they said)
10 O anthras moo lei oti... (he cannot come)
11 I Angela then erxete yati... (she works on a boat)
12 O filos moo lei oti... (you are very nice)
13 Episis lei oti... (he wants to have your phone number)
14 Ine kapios poo THeli na kseri... (what you did)
15 I mitera moo lei oti... (she likes the shops)
16 I fili moo then kseroon... (who took the car)
17 Kapios kseri... (how we can go to Thessaloniki)
18 Then ksero... (how much it costs to fix)

## Answers

1 Ne, to agorasa.
2 Then kanoone tipota.
3 Ton itha xTHes.
4 I ikoyenia moo meni eki.
5 I Elatha ine iperoxi.
6 i thiakopes teliosan.
7 tha pame stin Venetia too xronoo.
8 pote tha pate sto Los Angeles.
9 ti ipan.
10 then bori na erTHhi.
11 thoolevi se ena karavi.
12 isaste poli kalos.
13 THeli to noomero too tilefonoo sas.
14 ti kanate.
15 tis aresoon ta magazia.
16 pios pire to aftokinito.
17 pos pame stin THessaloniki.
18 poso kostizi na to ftiaksoone.

# Let's speak more Greek

◀) CD2, tr 26

## In your own words

This exercise will teach you to express yourself freely. Use only the words you have learned so far.

Tell me in your own words that...

1 next week it's back to work
2 you don't like to work; you'd rather have more holidays
3 nobody knows that you are in Athens
4 your mother has the number of your mobile phone
5 your vacation in Greece (Elatha) was wonderful
6 you did a lot of sightseeing and ate too much
7 your friend Andonis works for the Bank of Greece
8 he is catching a train to Larisa
9 your wife must go to Athens because her father is ill
10 you would like to go to Rhodes for Christmas, but by boat

### Answers

1 Tin epomeni evthomatha prepi na thoolepso/pao piso sti thoolia.
2 Then moo aresi i thoolia. Protimo na exo perisoteres diakopes.
3 Kanis then kseri oti ime stin ATHina.
4 I mitera moo exi to noomero too kinitoo tilefonoo moo.
5 I thiakopes moo/mas stin Elatha itan iperoxes.
6 Itha/ithame pola pragmata ke efaga/fagame para poli.
7 O filos moo/mas o Andonis thoolevi ya tin trapeza tis Elathos.
8 Perni to treno ya tin Larisa.
9 I yineka moo prepi na pai stin ATHina yati o pateras tis ine arostos.
10 THelo/THeloome na pao/pame stin Rotho ta Xristooyena,
    ala me karavi.

# Let's speak Greek – fast and fluently

🔊 CD2, tr 27

Translate each section and check if it is correct, then cover up the answers and say the three or four sentences fast!

Can you say them in just 20 seconds?

*My company can wait.*
*Nobody knows where I am.*
*My mother doesn't have the number of my mobile.*

I eteria moo bori na perimeni.
Kanis then kseri poo ime.
I mitera moo then exi to noomero too kinitoo moo.

*Next year I would like to go to Kos.*
*Kos at Christmas for a week? Are there any photos?*
*No, thank you. I don't see anything of interest.*

Too xronoo THelo na pao stin Ko.
Stin Ko ta Xristooyena ya mia evthomada? Exi fotografies?
Oxi, efxaristo. Then vlepo tipota enthiaferon.

*Hello, what are you doing here? What's the matter?*
*I need to repair my car and my flat. They are very old.*
*Can you help me, please – with 200 euros?*

Ya sas. Ti kanete etho? Ti simveni?
Prepi na ftiakso to aftokinito ke to thiamerisma moo. Ine poli palia.
Borite na me voiTHisete, parakalo – me thiakosia evro?

Now say all the sentences in Greek without stopping and starting.

# Test your progress

All 30 verbs have been included in this text! But don't panic –
it looks worse than it is. Go for it – you'll do brilliantly!

Translate into Greek:

1 We write many letters because we have a computer.
2 Hello, can I help? Your bag is not here? Where can it be?
3 Who knows his number? I am sorry, I don't know it.
4 How are you? I am happy that you do not smoke.
5 Do you want to see Sparti? It's a big town.
6 I do not like January. There is snow and it is often cold.
7 There is a kiosk down there. Would you like something to eat?
8 Why did they not phone? We waited until yesterday.
9 I took the book. He says it is interesting.
10 I believe that the airport is always open, day and night.
11 It is important to know (we) how much the client bought.
12 Have you seen the English newspaper? I do not like the photo.
   It is ugly.
13 He says that he has a cold. He thinks that he's coming tomorrow.
14 Is an apartment near the centre expensive in Greece?
15 We both have to work. Five children cost a lot.
16 I am going at Christmas. I have holidays in December and not (no)
   in July.
17 We know Pavlo very well. Do you like him?
18 Can you give me the dog? He is small but nice. What does he eat?
19 Her mother is here. She does not speak Greek. It is a little difficult
   for her.
20 Don't you know it? It costs 500 euros to fix (we).
21 I must go to the cashpoint machine. I need money.
22 I am sorry but **Fast Greek with Elisabeth Smith** is finished (teliose).

# Answers

## How to score

From a total of 100%:

- Subtract 1% for each wrong or missing word.
- Subtract 1% for the wrong form of the verb, like 'ime' when it should be '**imoon**' or '**imoona**' or '**boro pame**' instead of '**boro pao**'.

There are no penalties for:

- Wrong endings of words, like '**kalos**', when it should be '**kali**'.
- Picking the wrong word where there are two of similar meaning.
- Wrong word order.
- Wrong spelling, as long as you can say the word!
- Missing out odd little words which might not be translated in English, like '**na, i, to, tis, ton**', etc.

> **100% MINUS YOUR PENALTIES WILL GIVE YOU YOUR WEEKLY SCORE.**

For each test, correct your mistakes. Then read the corrected answers out loud twice.

## Week 1 – Test your progress

1 Kalimera, imaste o Ari ke i Jane.
2 Ime apo tin ATHina, ke esis?
3 Poo thoolevete tora?
4 Imoona stin ATHina ton Oktovrio.
5 I fili moo ine stin Elatha ya ena xrono.
6 Panda pame stin Rotho ton Ioonio.
7 Thoolepsa stin Fiat ton Maio.
8 Ti kanete sto Lonthino?
9 Thoolevo se ena skolio.
10 To megalo spiti sto Porto Rafti ine ya ta pethia.
11 Mia stigmi parakalo, poo ine o Aristotelis?
12 Exi to spiti tilefono? Thistixos oxi.
13 Kostizi poli mia Ferrari? Ne, vevea, kostizi para poli.
14 Pos ine i thoolia stin Elatha, kali?
15 O Aristotelis exi mia fili stin eteria moo.
16 Imaste stin Skiatho tris meres tora.
17 Exoome kales THesis sto aeroplano.
18 Panda exo varetes thiakopes.
19 Exi mia omorfi yineka, mia Lamborghini ke pola lefta.
20 Isaste i kiria Onassis? Exete ena megalo aeroplano.

Your score: _____ %

## Week 2 – Test your progress

1 Poo ine ena tilefono?
2 Signomi, exoome mono pistotikes kartes.
3 Boroome na pame stis epta avrio?
4 Exete ena arketa megalo trapezi? Imaste pende.
5 Ta mikra thomatia then exoone banio.
6 THeloome na fame zambon ke psomakia.
7 Boroome na pame apo tis eksi mexri tis epta para tetarto.
8 Poo boroome na pioome kati etho konda?
9 Imaste sto bar apo tis enea mexri tis theka ke misi.
10 Endaksi, pernoome to Rover ya mia mera.
11 Poso kostizi to proino? Mono theka evro.
12 Ti THelete? To komputer? Then thoolevi.

94

13 Pos ine i milopita? Kali ala akrivi.

14 Poo ine i tooaletes, aristera i theksia?

15 Boro na pao sto Holliwood.

16 Ena kafe parakalo… pinoome para poli kafe!

17 Poo ine i kiria Pavlithi? Isos sto bar?

18 Eksi evro ya ena krio tsai? Ine ligo akrivo.

19 Imoona stin Rotho ton Fevrooario. Then ine asxima.

20 Ine triakosia bar etho, ena ine trianda metra theksia.

> **Your score:** _____ %

## Week 3 – Test your progress

1 Prota THelo na pao stin mixani analipsis.

2 Se afto to magazi ta papootsia kostizoone para poli.

3 Ithate ton anthra moo sto farmakio?

4 Imaste etho mexri tis theka ke tetarto.

5 Ithame to tenis stin Anglia stin tileorasi.

6 Lipame ala then exoome to ithio se kokino, se noomero sarandatesera.

7 Afto to magazi then ine ftino.

8 Pios eftiakse to tilefono moo? Esis?

9 Etho ine to polikatastima. Ala then ine anixto.

10 Simera then agorasame para pola pragmata. Mono psomi ke miso kilo vootiro.

11 Ta efaga ola – avga, mila, patates ke ena komati tiri.

12 Prepi na kanoome ta psonia. Ine afto to kendro?

13 XTHes imoona stin eteria mexri tis enea.

14 I Anglikes efimerithes kostizoon poli stin Elatha.

15 Exi leoforio? Oxi? Then pirazi.

16 Itan enas poli kalos politis.

17 Ti ine afto? Kati ya mena?

18 Agorase tin tsanda etho konda i sto Notos Galleries?

19 Ola itane poli akriva. Etsi then agorasa tipota.

20 Xriazomaste tria kila, pistevo.

> **Your score:** _____ %

## Week 4 – Test your progress

1 Kapios tilefonise ston kirio Thiamandi?
2 THelo na ksero poo ine to estiatorio.
3 Ine arga ke then ine eki. Ti kanoome apopse?
4 Etho ine to menoo! Kserete ta krasia tis Axaias?
5 I mixani analipsis ine epano, piso apo tin eksotho, thipla stin porta.
6 Tin Tetarti prepi na pame ston yatro. Ine ena simandiko randevoo.
7 Yati leo oti ine vareti? Yati tin ksero kala.
8 Ton ithate? Prepi na pao stin Larisa mazi too.
9 O kirios Thiamandis ine pelatis moo. Ta agorase ola.
10 THelo na agoraso afto to pragma. Pos lene sta Elinika…?
11 Tin epomeni evthomatha? Lipame. Then ine thinaton.
12 Borite na me voiTHisete parakalo. Efxaristo poli!
13 Triakosia evro ya thio meres. Poli enthiaferon. Ne, fisika to pernoome.
14 Prepi na agoraso tria pragmata ya toos filoos moo.
15 Exo krioma. Xriazome ena yatro.
16 Boroone na fane mono ton baklava?
17 Ine enas apesios skilos. Ti boroome na kanoome?
18 Kanis then ithe pios efaye tin brizola.
19 Boro na po kati: to kotopoolo then ine asximo, ala to psari ine kalitero.
20 Ti pernete? Ta froota? Ne, vevea, ine apo tin Axaia.

Your score: _____ %

## Week 5 – Test your progress

1 Apagorevete na pate sto estiatorio xoris papootsia.
2 Moo aresi i Porsche sas. Itan poli ftini?
3 Otan ime se thiakopes milao Elinika poli.
4 Xriazome eksi isitiria. Exete mi-kapnizondes THesis?
5 Pistevo oti exoome provlimata me tin mixani.
6 Then moo aresi to Internet. Ine poli thiskolo.
7 Then katalaveno. Borite na milate pio arga parakalo?
8 Kani zesti ke exi kosmo. Pame stin poli.
9 Mia ora mazi tis moo thini ponokefalo.
10 Sta fanaria ine ena leoforio. Poo pai?
11 I pistotiki karta then ine etho. Prepi na tilefonisoome stin astinomia.
12 As to kanoome etsi: prota agorazoome to Ferrari ya mena ke meta to bloozaki ya sena.

13 Moo aresi afto to aftokinito ala to alo itan kalitero.

14 Exoome mono ena litro venzini ke then exi venzinathiko mexri tin ATHina.

15 Moo aresi o ilios ke moo aresi i vroxi. Moo aresoon ke ta thio.

16 Parakalo, imaste ikosi xiliometra apo tin ATHina. Exi kanena garaz?

17 Signomi. Xriazome voithia parakalo. Then ksero tin ATHina. Poo ine o staTHmos?

18 O kendrikos thromos? Then ine poli thiskolo. An pernete ton ipoyio.

19 Poo ine? Ti ekanan? Then moo aresi na perimeno.

20 Erxomaste apo tin platforma thekaepta. Poo ine o Spiros?

Your score: _____ %

## Week 6 – Test your progress

1 Grafoome pola gramata yati exoome ena komputer.

2 Yasas, boro na voiTHiso? I tsanda sas then ine etho? Poo bori na ine?

3 Pios kseri to noomero too? Lipame, then to ksero.

4 Ti kanete? Ime ikanopioimenos poo then kapnizete alo.

5 THelete na thite tin Sparti? Ine mia megali poli.

6 Then moo aresi o lanooarios. Exi xioni ke sixna kani krio.

7 Ine ena periptero eki kato. THelete kati na fate?

8 Yati then tilefonisan? Perimename mexri xTHes.

9 Pira to vivlio. Lei oti ine poli enthiaferon.

10 Pistevo oti to aerothromio ine panda anixto, mera ke nixta.

11 Ine simandiko na kseroome poso agorase o pelatis.

12 Ithes tin Angliki efimeritha? Then moo aresi i fotografia. Ine asximi.

13 Lei oti exi krioma. Pistevi oti erxete avrio.

14 Ine ena thiamerisma konda sto kendro akrivo stin Elatha?

15 Ke i thio prepi na thoolepsoome. Pende pethia kostizoon poli.

16 Piyeno ta Xristooyena. Exo tis thiakopes ton Thekemvrio ke oxi ton loolio.

17 Kseroome ton Pavlo poli kala. Sas aresi?

18 Borite na moo thosete ton skilo? Ine mikros ala kalos. Ti troi?

19 I mitera tis ine etho. Then milai Elinika. Ine ligo thiskolo ya aftin.

20 Then to kseris? Kostizi pendakosia evro na to ftiaksoome.

21 Prepi na pao stin mixani analipsis. Xriazome lefta.

22 Lipame ala to **Fast Greek with Elisabeth Smith** teliose.

## Say it simply (Week 6)

1 Signomi, exo ena megalo provlima. Isos ine kokino krasi. Ala then ime veveos. Imaste sto ksenothoxio mexri avrio. Pame stin ATHina stis epta. Borite na to kanete simera parakalo?

2 Parakalo. Kalimera, ime i Kate Walker. Tilefono apo to aerothromio. Imoona sto thomatio ikosithio ya tris meres. Lipame ala ine pragmata sto thomatio ke tora ime sto aerothromio ke pame sto Birmingham. Borite na me voiTHisete parakalo? To ksenothoxio kseri poo meno sto Birmingham. Efxaristo poli.

## Spot the keys (Week 6)

It depends when you are going. Normally it takes 20 minutes. But if there is a lot of traffic and a queue on the bridge, it takes at least 35 minutes. You can read the price on the meter. It will be between 60 and 70 euros.

# Greek–English dictionary

In this section you'll find all the **New words** that you have learned, including the 'extras', in alphabetical order. To make it easy for you to find what you may have forgotten, words are shown exactly as they appear in the **New words** section. For example, if you learned *a lot* you'll find it under 'a'. If you don't remember how to say *I work* you'll find it under 'I'.

adio *goodbye*
aerothromio *airport*
aftokinito *car*
aftokinitothromos *motorway*
aftos/i/o *this*
agorasa *I bought, I have bought*
agoraso *I buy*
agorasoome *we buy*
akrivo *expensive*
ala *but*
alfa *a*
alo *other*
Amerikana *American*
Anglia *England*
anixta *open*
anthras *husband/man*
apagorevete to kapnisma
   *it's forbidden to smoke*
apesio *terrible*
apo *from*
apopse *tonight*
Aprilio(s) *April*
arga *late; slow(ly)*
argotera *later*
aristera *left*
arithmi *numbers*
arketa *enough*
arostos/i *sick*
as elpisume *let's hope*
aspros/i/o *white*
astinomia *police*

avgo/a *egg/eggs*
Avgoosto/s *August*
avrio *tomorrow*

baklavas *famous Greek pastry*
banio *bath*
bira/es *beer/beers*
ble *blue*
bloozaki *T-shirt*
bookali *bottle*
bori (na ftiaksi…) *he/she/
   it can (fix…)*
bori na perimeni *it can wait*
borite na me voithisete *can you
   help me?*
borite na milisete…? *can you
   speak…?*
boroome (na) *we can*
brizola *steak*
brosta *in front of*

doosh *shower*

efimeritha, mia *a newspaper*
efxaristo *thank you*
efxaristo poli *thank you very much*
egrapsa *I wrote*
ekato *hundred/a hundred*
eki *there*
eki kato *down there*
eki pera *over there*

**99**

eklisia *church*
eksi *six*
eksinda *sixty*
eksothos *exit*
eksoxa *wonderful*
ela!/elate! *come! (familiar/formal)*
emina *I lived*
ena *one*
ena lepto *a minute (just a minute)*
enas minas *a month*
enas xronos *a year*
enas/mia/ena *a/one*
endaksi *all right, OK*
enea *nine*
eneninda *ninety*
entheka *eleven*
enthiaferon, enthiaferoosa *interesting*
epano *up/upstairs*
epithorpio *dessert*
epta *seven*
erxomaste *we come/we're coming*
esis *you*
estiatorio *restaurant*
eteria *company/firm*
etho *here*
etsi *therefore, in that case*
evro *euro, euros*
evthomatha, mia *a week*
evthominda *seventy*
exi *he/she/it has*
exi kosmo *it's crowded*
exo *I have*
exoome *we have*

fagame *we ate, have eaten*
fanaria *lights*
fandastikos/i/o *fantastic*
farmakio *chemist's*
Fevrooarios *February*
fili *(girl)friend*
fisika *of course/naturally*
fotografia *photograph*
froota *fruit*
**100** ftino *cheap*

gala *milk*
garaz *garage*
grafo *I write*
grafoome *we write*
gramaria *grams*
gramata *letters*
gramatokivotio *letter box*
gramatosima *stamps*
gri *grey*
grigora *quickly*

i *the, or*
i nixta *the night*
i ora *the time*
i thoolia *the work*
i tileorasi *the television*
i tooaleta, tooaletes *the toilet(s)*
i Trapeza tis Elathos *the Bank of Greece*
Ianooarios *January*
ikanopioimenos/i/o *satisfied, happy*
ikosi *twenty*
ikosiena *twenty one*
ikosithio *twenty two*
ikositria *twenty three*
ikoyenia *family*
ilios *the sun*
imaste *we are, we were/ have been*
ime *I am*
imoon, imoona *I was*
ine *he/she/it is*
ine mia *it's one o'clock*
ine thio *it's two o'clock*
Ioolios *July*
Ioonios *June*
ipe *he/she/it said*
iperoxos/i/o *wonderful*
ipoyio *underground*
isaste *you are/are you?*
isia *straight on*
isitirio *ticket*
isos *perhaps*
itan *was/were*
itha *I saw*

kafe *brown*
kafes/kafe *coffee*
kakos/ia/o *bad*
kala *well*
kalimera *good morning*
kalinixta *good night*
kalispera *good evening*
kalitera *better*
kalos/kali/kalo *good, nice*
kane grigora! *hurry up!*
kanena *none/any (things)*
kanete *you do/do you do?*
kani krio *it is cold*
kanis *nobody/anyone*
kanoome *do (we)*
kanoone *they do/make*
kapion *someone*
kapios *someone*
kapnizi *he/she/it smokes*
karavi *boat*
kart-postal *postcard*
katharos/i/o *clean*
kati *something*
kati na fate *something to eat*
ke *and/past (with time)*
ke esis *and you?/you, too?*
ke misi *half past*
ke ta thio *both (and the two)*
ke tetarto *quarter past*
ke tote? *and then?*
kendrikos thromos *main road (central road)*
kendro *centre*
kenooryios/a/o *new*
kero *time*
keros *weather/time*
kilo *kilo*
kinito *mobile phone*
kiria *Mrs/lady*
Kiriaki *Sunday*
kirios *Mr/gentleman*
kitrino *yellow*
kokino *red*
komati *piece*
konda *near*
kostizi *it costs*

kostizoon *they cost*
kotopoolo *chicken*
krasi *wine*
kreas *meat*
krioma *cold/flu*
krios/a/o *cold*
kseri *he/she/it knows*
ksero *I know*
kseroome *we know*

lathi *oil*
laxanika *vegetables*
lefta *money*
lei *he/she says*
leoforio *bus*
lepto/lepta *minute, minutes*
ligo *little*
lipame *I'm sorry*
lipon *well…*
litro *litre*
logariasmos *bill*

magazi, magazia *shop, shops*
Maios *May*
Martios *March*
mas *our*
mavro *black*
mazi too *with him*
me *with*
me epistrofi *(with) return*
megalo *big*
mena *me*
meni *he/she/it lives or stays*
meno *I live*
menoo *menu*
mera, meres *day, days*
mera, mia *a day*
meres tis evthomatas *days of the week*
meriki/es/a *some, several*
meta *then*
meta *then, afterwards*
metra *metres*
mexri *until*
mi kapnizondes *non-smoking*
mia *a, an*

**101**

mias katefTHinsis *one way*
mikros/i/o *small*
milane *they speak*
milao *I speak*
milopita *apple pie*
mines *months*
miso/misi *half*
mitera *mother*
mithen *zero*
mixani *machine/engine*
mixani analipsis *cashpoint machine*
mono *only*
moo *my*
moo aresi *I like*

na exoome proino *to have breakfast (we)*
na pyite *to drink*
ne *yes*
nero *water*
Noemvrios *November*
noomero *size, number*
nosokomio *hospital*

o *the*
ogthonda *eighty*
okto *eight*
Oktovrios *October*
ola, oli, olo, oles, olos *all*
omorfos/i/o *beautiful*
ora, mia *an hour*
otan *when*
oti *that*
oxi *no*
oxi asximo/a *not bad*

pagoto *ice cream*
palios/ia/io *old (things)*
pame *we/let's go*
panda *always*
pao *I go, I'm going*
para *less/before (with time)*
para pola *too many*
para poli *too much*
para tetarto *quarter to*
parakalo *please*

Paraskevi *Friday*
patates *potatoes*
patates tiganites *chips*
pelatis *client*
Pempti *Thursday*
pende *five*
peninda *fifty*
perimene/perimenete *wait! (familiar/formal)*
perimeno *I wait*
periptero *kiosk (it sells stamps)*
pernoome *we take*
pethia *children*
pio *more*
piome *drink (we)*
pios, pia, pio *who, which*
piso apo *behind*
pistevi *he/she/it believes*
pistevo *I believe/think*
pistotikes kartes *credit cards*
platforma *platform*
poli *city/town, also: very, much, a lot, many*
polikatastima *department store*
politis *sales assistant*
pono *pain*
ponokefalo *headache*
poo *where*
porta *door*
portokali *orange*
pos *how*
Pos lene sta Elinika...? *How do you say in Greek...?*
posa *how many*
poses *how many*
posi *how many*
poso kostizi *how much does it cost?*
pote *when?*
pote *never/ever*
pothosfero *football*
potiri *glass*
pragma *thing*
pragmata *things*
prasino *green*
prepi na *we must*
proino *breakfast*

prota *first*
protimisa *I preferred*
protimo *I prefer*
proto *first*
provlima *problem*
psari *fish*
psito *grilled*
psomaki, psomakia *bread rolls*
psomi *bread*

randevoo *appointment*
roz *pink*

salata *salad*
san *like*
saranda *forty*
saravalo *wreck*
Savato *Saturday*
se *in, at*
se thiakopes *on holiday*
Septemvrios *September*
servitoros *waiter*
signomi *excuse me*
simandiko *important*
simera *today*
sinexia *always*
sixna *often*
skilos *dog*
skolio *school*
soovlaki *Greek meat dish*
spiti *house*
sta Anglika *in English*
stasi *(bus) stop*
stathmos *(railway) station*
stegnokatharistirio *dry cleaner's*
stigmi, mia *one moment*
stin *at*
stis *in the*
stis pende? *at five o'clock?*
sto *to*
sto aeroplano *in the aeroplane*
sto bar *in the bar*

ta *the*
ta papootsia *the shoes*
ta psonia *the shopping*

Ta xromata *colours*
taksithevondas *on the move/travelling*
taxithromio *post office*
telefteo *last*
teliosame *we finished/we've finished*
teliosan *are finished*
tesera *four*
Tetarti *Wednesday*
tetarto *quarter*
THee moo! *good grief!*
Theftera *Monday*
theftero *second*
theka *ten*
thekaeksi *sixteen*
thekaenea *nineteen*
thekaepta *seventeen*
thekaokto *eighteen*
thekapende *fifteen*
thekatesera *fourteen*
thekatria *thirteen*
Thekemvrios *December*
theksia *right*
THelo *I want*
THeloome (na) *we want/we'd like*
then *not*
then katalaveno *I don't understand*
then moo aresi *I don't like*
then pirazi *it doesn't matter*
then THA exoome *we won't have*
THesi, THesis *seat, seats*
thiakosia *two hundred*
thiamerisma *apartment*
thiklino *double room*
thinaton *possible*
thio *two*
thipla *by, next to*
thiskolos/i/o *difficult*
thistixos *unfortunately*
thomatio *room*
thoolepsa *I worked*
thoolevete *you work/do you work?*
thoolevo *I work*
thotheka *twelve*
ti *what*
ti kanete? *How are you?*
ti ora? *at what time?*

ti simveni? *what's the matter?*
ti thelete? *what would you like?*
tilefonise *(has) telephoned*
tin *the*
tin epomeni evthomatha *next week*
tiri *cheese*
tis *the*
to *the*
to ithio *the same*
to komotirio *the hairdresser's*
to Notos Galleries *a well-known Greek department store*
to tilefono *the telephone*
ton *the*
too *of*
too xronoo *next year*
tora *now*
trapezi *table*
trelos/i/o *crazy*
treno *train*
tria *three*
trianda *thirty*
Triti *Tuesday*
trome *we eat*
tsai *tea*
tsanda *bag*

valitsa *suitcase*
varetos/i/o *boring*
venzinathiko *petrol station*

venzini *petrol*
vevea *sure, certain(ly)*
vita *b*
vivlio *book*
vlepo *I see*
voithiso *to help*
vootiro *butter*
vroxi rain *(vr exi – it's raining)*

xartis, xarti *map*
xilia *thousand*
xiliometro *kilometre*
xioni *snow*
xoris *without*
xriazome *I need*
Xristooyena *Christmas*
xrono, xronia *year, years*
xTHes *yesterday*

ya *for*
ya/yasoo (sing.)/yasas (pl.)
   *hello, goodbye/bye*
yati *why*
yatros *doctor*
yematos/i/o *full*
yineka *woman, wife*

zambon *ham*
zaxari *sugar*
zesti *hot*

# English–Greek dictionary

*a* alfa
*a lot* poli
*a* enas/mia/ena
*afterwards* meta
*airport* aerothromio
*all* olos, oli, olo, oles, ola
*all right* endaksi
*always* panda, sinexia
*American* Amerikana
*and* ke
*and then?* ke tote?
*and you?/you, too?* ke esis?
*and/past (with time)* ke
*apartment* thiamerisma
*apple pie* milopita
*appointment* randevoo
*April* Aprilio(s)
*are finished* teliosan
*are you?* isaste
*at* stin/se
*at five o'clock?* stis pende?
*at what time?* ti ora?
*August* Avgoosto/s

*b* vita
*bad* kakos/ia/o
*bag* tsanda
*bath* banio
*beautiful* omorfos/i/o
*beer/beers* bira/es
*behind* piso apo
*better* kalitera
*big* megalo
*bill* logariasmos
*black* mavro
*blue* ble

*boat* karavi
*book* vivlio
*boring* varetos/i/o
*both (and the two)* ke ta thio
*bottle* bookali
*bread* psomi
*bread roll/rolls (little/small bread)*
    psomaki, psomakia
*breakfast* proino
*brown* kafe
*bus* leoforio
*bus stop* stasi
*but* ala
*butter* vootiro
*by* thipla

*can you help me?* borite na me
    voithisete
*can you speak ...?* borite na
    milisete ...?
*car* aftokinito
*cashpoint machine* mixani
    analipsis
*centre* kendro
*cheap* ftino
*cheese* tiri
*chemist's* farmakio
*chicken* kotopoolo
*children* pethia
*chips* patates tiganites
*Christmas* Xristooyena
*church* eklisia
*city* poli
*clean* katharos/i/o
*client* pelatis
*coffee* kafes/kafe

*cold* krios/a/o (adj), krioma (noun)
*colours* Ta xromata
*come! (familiar/formal)* ela!/elate!
*company* eteria
*crazy* trelos/i/o
*credit cards* pistotikes kartes

*day, a/days* mia mera/meres
*days of the week* meres tis
   evthomatas
*December* Thekemvrios
*department store* polikatastima
*dessert* epithorpio
*difficult* thiskolos/i/o
*do (we)* kanoome
*do you work?* thoolevete
*doctor* yatros
*dog* skilos
*door* porta
*double room* thiklino
*down there* eki kato
*drink, to drink* na pyite
*drink (we)* piooome
*dry cleaner's* stegnokatharistirio

*egg/eggs* avgo/a
*eight* okto
*eighteen* thekaokto
*eighty* ogthonda
*eleven* entheka
*engine* mixani
*England* Anglia
*enough* arketa
*euro, euros* evro
*excuse me* signomi
*exit* eksothos
*expensive* akrivo

*family* ikoyenia
*famous Greek pastry* baklavas
*fantastic* fandastikos/i/o
*February* Fevrooarios
*fifteen* thekapende
*fifty* peninda

*firm* eteria
*first* prota/proto
*fish* psari
*five* pende
*flu* krioma
*football* pothosfero
*for* ya
*forty* saranda
*four* tesera
*fourteen* thekatesera
*Friday* Paraskevi
*from* apo
*fruit* froota
*full* yematos/i/o

*garage (car mechanic's garage)*
   garaz
*girl friend* fili
*glass* potiri
*good evening* kalispera
*good grief!* THee moo!
*good morning* kalimera
*good night* kalinixta
*good, nice* kalos/kali/kalo
*goodbye* adio
*grams* gramaria
*Greek meat dish (like shish kebab)*
   soovlaki
*green* prasino
*grey* gri
*grilled* psito

*hairdresser's, the* to komotirio
*half* miso/misi
*half past* ke misi
*ham* zambon
*happy* ikanopioimenos/i/o
*has telephoned* tilefonise
*have breakfast, to have breakfast (we)*
   na exoome proino
*he believes* pistevi
*he can (fix…)* bori (na ftiaksi…)
*he has* exi
*he is* ine

*he knows* kseri
*he lives or stays* meni
*he said* ipe
*he says* lei
*he smokes* kapnizi
*headache* ponokefalo
*hello, goodbye/bye* ya/yasoo (sing.)/ yasas (pl.)
*help, to help* voithiso
*here* etho
*hospital* nosokomio
*hot* zesti
*hour, an* mia ora
*house* spiti
*how* pos
*How are you?* ti kanete?
*How do you say in Greek …?* Pos lene sta Elinika …
*how many* posi/poses/posa
*how much does it cost?* poso kostizi
*hundred/a hundred* ekato
*hurry up!* kane grigora!
*husband* anthras

*I am* ime
*I believe* pistevo
*I bought* agorasa
*I buy* agoraso
*I don't like* then moo aresi
*I don't understand* then katalaveno
*I go* pao
*I have* exo
*I have bought* agorasa
*I know* ksero
*I like* moo aresi
*I live* meno
*I lived* emina
*I need* xriazome
*I prefer* protimo
*I preferred* protimisa
*I saw* itha
*I see* vlepo
*I speak* milao
*I think* pistevo

*I wait* perimeno
*I want* THelo
*I was* imoon/imoona
*I work* thoolevo
*I worked* thoolepsa
*I write* grafo
*I wrote* egrapsa
*I'm going* pao
*I'm sorry* lipame
*ice cream* pagoto
*important* simandiko
*in* se
*in English* sta Anglika
*in front of* brosta
*in that case* etsi
*in the* stis
*in the aeroplane* sto aeroplano
*in the bar* sto bar
*interesting* enthiaferon/enthiaferoosa
*it believes* pistevi
*it can (fix…)* bori (na ftiaksi…)
*it can wait* bori na perimeni
*it costs* kostizi
*it doesn't matter* then pirazi
*it has* exi
*it is* ine
*it is cold (lit. it makes cold)* kani krio
*it knows* kseri
*it lives or stays* meni
*it said* ipe
*it smokes* kapnizi
*it's crowded* exi kosmo
*it's forbidden to smoke* apagorevete to kapnisma
*it's one o'clock* ine mia
*it's two o'clock* ine thio

*January* Ianooarios
*July* Ioolios
*June* Ioonios

*kilo* kilo
*kilometre* xiliometro
*kiosk (it sells stamps)* periptero

*last* telefteo
*late/slow(ly)* arga
*later* argotera
*left* aristera
*less/before (with time)* para
*let's hope* as elpisume
*letter box* gramatokivotio
*letters* gramata
*lights (also used for traffic lights)* fanaria
*like* san
*litre* litro
*little* ligo

*machine* mixani
*main road (central road)* kendrikos thromos
*man* anthras
*map* xartis, xarti
*March* Martios
*May* Maios
*me* mena
*meat* kreas
*menu* menoo
*metres* metra
*milk* gala
*minute, a (also: just a minute)/ minutes* ena lepto/lepta
*mobile phone* kinito
*Monday* Theftera
*money* lefta
*month, a* enas minas
*months* mines
*more* pio
*mother* mitera
*motorway* aftokinitothromos
*Mr/gentleman* kirios
*Mrs/lady* kiria
*much* poli
*my* moo

*naturally* fisika
*near* konda
*never/ever* pote

*new* kenooryios/a/o
*newspaper, a* mia efimeritha
*next to* thipla
*next week* tin epomeni evthomatha
*next year* too xronoo
*nice, good* kalos/kali/kalo
*night, the* i nixta
*nine* enea
*nineteen* thekaenea
*ninety* eneninda
*no* oxi
*nobody/anyone* kanis
*none/any (things)* kanena
*non-smoking* mi kapnizondes
*not* then
*not at all (and what you say when answering the phone)* parakalo
*not bad* oxi asximo/a
*November* Noemvrios
*now* tora
*number* noomero
*numbers (list of numbers)* arithmi

*October* Oktovrios
*of* too
*of course* fisika
*often* sixna
*oil* lathi
*OK* endaksi
*old (things)* palios/ia/io
*on holiday* se thiakopes
*on the move/travelling* taksithevondas
*one* ena
*one moment* mia stigmi
*one way* mias katefTHinsis
*only* mono
*open* anixta
*or* i
*orange* portokali
*other* alo
*our* mas
*over there* eki pera

| | |
|---|---|
| *pain* pono | *she knows* kseri |
| *perhaps* isos | *she lives or stays* meni |
| *petrol* venzini | *she said* ipe |
| *petrol station* venzinathiko | *she says* lei |
| *photograph* fotografia | *she smokes* kapnizi |
| *piece* komati | *shoes, the* ta papootsia |
| *pink* roz | *shop, shops* magazi, magazia |
| *platform* platforma | *shopping, the* ta psonia |
| *please* parakalo | *shower* doosh |
| *police* astinomia | *sick* arostos/i |
| *possible* thinaton | *six* eksi |
| *post office* taxithromio | *sixteen* thekaeksi |
| *postcard* kart-postal | *sixty* eksinda |
| *potatoes* patates | *size* noomero |
| *problem* provlima | *small* mikros/i/o |
| | *snow* xioni |
| *quarter* tetarto | *some, several* meriki/es/a |
| *quarter past* ke tetarto | *someone* kapios/kapion |
| *quarter to* para tetarto | *something* kati |
| *quickly* grigora | *something to eat* kati na fate |
| | *stamps* gramatosima |
| *railway station* stathmos | *steak* brizola |
| *rain* vroxi | *straight on* isia |
| *red* kokino | *sugar* zaxari |
| *restaurant* estiatorio | *suitcase* valitsa |
| *right* theksia | *sun, the* ilios |
| *room* thomatio | *Sunday* Kiriaki |
| | *sure, certain(ly)* vevea |
| *salad* salata | |
| *sales assistant* politis | *table* trapezi |
| *same, the* to ithio | *tea* tsai |
| *satisfied* ikanopioimenos/i/o | *telephone, the* to tilefono |
| *Saturday* Savato | *television, the* i tileorasi |
| *school* skolio | *ten* theka |
| *seat, seats* THesi, THesis | *terrible* apesio |
| *second* theftero | *thank you, thank you very much* |
| *September* Septemvrios | efxaristo, efxaristo poli |
| *seven* epta | *that* oti |
| *seventeen* thekaepta | *the* o/i/to/ta/tis/tin/ton |
| *seventy* evthominda | *the Bank of Greece* i Trapeza tis |
| *she believes* pistevi | Elathos |
| *she can (fix…)* bori (na ftiaksi…) | *then* meta |
| *she has* exi | *there* eki |
| *she is* ine | *therefore* etsi |

*they cost* kostizoon
*they do* kanoone
*they make* kanoone
*they speak* milane
*thing/s* pragma/pragmata
*thirteen* thekatria
*thirty* trianda
*this* aftos/i/o
*thousand* xilia
*three* tria
*Thursday* Pempti
*ticket* isitirio
*time* kero/keros
*time, the (telling the time)* i ora
*to* sto
*today* simera
*toilet(s), the* i tooaleta, tooaletes
*tomorrow* avrio
*tonight* apopse
*too many* para pola
*too much* para poli
*town* poli
*train* treno
*T-shirt* bloozaki
*Tuesday* Triti
*twelve* thotheka
*twenty* ikosi
*twenty-one* ikosiena
*twenty-three* ikositria
*twenty-two* ikosithio
*two* thio
*two hundred* thiakosia

*underground* ipoyio
*unfortunately* thistixos
*until* mexri
*up* epano
*upstairs* epano

*vegetables* laxanika
*very* poli

*wait! (familiar/formal)* perimene/ perimenete

*waiter* servitoros
*was* itan
*water* nero
*we are, we were/have been* imaste/imastan
*we ate, have eaten* fagame
*we buy* agorasoome
*we can* boroome (na)
*we come* erxomaste
*we eat* trome
*we have* exoome
*we know* kseroome
*we must* prepi na
*we take* pernoome
*we want/we'd like* theloome (na)
*we won't have* then tha exoome
*we write* grafoome
*we/let's go* pame
*we're coming* erxomaste
*we've finished/we finished* teliosame
*weather* keros
*Wednesday* Tetarti
*week, a* mia evthomatha
*well* kala
*well...* lipon
*well-known Greek department store, a* to Notos Galleries
*were* itan
*what* ti
*what would you like? (lit. what (do) you want?)* ti thelete?
*what's the matter?* ti simveni?
*when* otan
*when?* pote
*where* poo
*which, who* pios, pia, pio
*white* aspros/i/o
*who?, which?* pios?, pia?, pio?
*why* yati
*wife* yineka
*wine* krasi
*with* me
*with him* mazi too

*with return* me epistrofi
*without* xoris
*woman* yineka
*wonderful* iperoxos/i/o
*work, the* i thoolia
*wreck* saravalo

*year, a* enas xronos
*year, years* xrono, xronia

*yellow* kitrino
*yes* ne
*yesterday* xTHes
*you* esis
*you are* isaste
*you do* kanete
*you work* thoolevete

*zero* mithen

# How to use the flash cards

Learning words and sentences can be tedious, but with flash cards it's quick and good fun.

## This is what you do

When the **Day-by-day** guide tells you to use the cards, cut them out, photocopy them or copy them on to card. There are 24 **Flash words** and 10 **Flash sentences** for each week. Each card has a little number on it telling you to which week it belongs, so you won't cut out too many cards at a time or muddle them up later on.

First, try to learn the words and sentences by looking at both sides of the cards. Then, when you have a rough idea, start testing yourself. That's the fun bit. Look at the English, say the Greek, and then check. Make three piles: for the 'correct', 'wrong' and 'don't know' ones. When all the cards are used up, start again with the 'wrong' pile and try to whittle it down until you get all of them right. You can also play it 'backwards' by starting with the Greek face-up.

Keep the cards in a little box or put an elastic band around them. Take them with you on the bus, the train, to the hairdresser's or the dentist's. Do a quick 'turn and learn' whenever you have a bit of spare time.

The 24 **Flash words** for each week are there to start you off. Convert the rest of the **New words** to **Flash words**, too. It's well worth it!

> **Flash cards for 'fast' learning:**
> **Don't lose them – use them!**

| exoome 1 | ne 1 |
| parakalo 1 | imaste 1 |
| trapeza<br>ΤΡΑΠΕΖΑ 1 | pame 1 |
| pao 1 | apo 1 |
| imoona 1 | ine 1 |
| poli 1 | omorfos 1 |

Cut out and use ✂

| yes [1] | we have [1] |
|---|---|
| we are, we were [1] | please [1] |
| we/let's go [1] | bank [1] |
| from [1] | I go, I'm going [1] |
| he/she/it is [1] | I was [1] |
| beautiful [1] | very, much, a lot [1] |

Cut out and use ✂

| ti <sup>1</sup> | poo <sup>1</sup> |
| exo <sup>1</sup> | tora <sup>1</sup> |
| kalispera <sup>1</sup> | kalos/kali/ kalo <sup>1</sup> |
| signomi <sup>1</sup> | ime <sup>1</sup> |
| ya <sup>1</sup> | i thoolia <sup>1</sup> |
| xrono <sup>1</sup> | lefta <sup>1</sup> |

Cut out and use ✂

| where [1] | what [1] |
|---|---|
| now [1] | I have [1] |
| good, nice [1] | good evening [1] |
| I am [1] | excuse me [1] |
| the work [1] | for [1] |
| money [1] | year [1] |

Cut out and use ✂

| 2 | 2 |
|---|---|
| **ligo** | **etho** |
| 2 | 2 |
| **aristera** | **arketa** |
| 2 | 2 |
| **ala** | **poso kostizi?** |
| 2 | 2 |
| **oxi** | **proino** |
| 2 | 2 |
| **endaksi** | **avrio** |
| 2 | 2 |
| **kati** | **mono** |

Cut out and use ✂

| | |
|---|---|
| **here** 2 | **little** 2 |
| **enough** 2 | **left** 2 |
| **how much?** 2 | **but** 2 |
| **breakfast** 2 | **no** 2 |
| **tomorrow** 2 | **OK** 2 |
| **only** 2 | **something** 2 |

Cut out and use ✂

| 2 | 2 |
|---|---|
| **theksia** | **ke** |

| 2 | 2 |
|---|---|
| **isia** | **tsai** |

| 2 | 2 |
|---|---|
| **logariasmos** | **akrivo** |

| 2 | 2 |
|---|---|
| **thiklino** | **micros/i/o** |

| 2 | 2 |
|---|---|
| **oxi asximo** | **pistotikes kartes** |

| 2 | 2 |
|---|---|
| **krios/a/o** | **konda** |

| and 2 | right 2 |
| tea 2 | straight on 2 |
| expensive 2 | bill 2 |
| small 2 | double room 2 |
| credit cards 2 | not bad 2 |
| near 2 | cold 2 |

Cut out and use ✂

| | |
|---|---|
| 3<br><br>**simera** | 3<br><br>**prepi** |
| 3<br><br>**lipame** | 3<br><br>**leoforio** |
| 3<br><br>**taxithromio**<br>**ΤΑΧΥΔΡΟΜΕΙΟ** | 3<br><br>**olo** |
| 3<br><br>**meta** | 3<br><br>**THelo** |
| 3<br><br>**magazi** | 3<br><br>**mexri** |
| 3<br><br>**pote** | 3<br><br>**argotera** |

| 3 | 3 |
|---|---|
| **must** | **today** |
| 3 | 3 |
| **bus** | **I'm sorry** |
| 3 | 3 |
| **all** | **post office** |
| 3 | 3 |
| **I want** | **after, afterwards** |
| 3 | 3 |
| **until** | **shop** |
| 3 | 3 |
| **later** | **when** |

Cut out and use ✂

| | |
|---|---|
| 3<br><br>**etho** | 3<br><br>**komati** |
| 3<br><br>**xTHes** | 3<br><br>**periptero** |
| 3<br><br>**pios** | 3<br><br>**afto** |
| 3<br><br>**kakos/ia/o** | 3<br><br>**tiri** |
| 3<br><br>**psomi** | 3<br><br>**ftino** |
| 3<br><br>**pragmata** | 3<br><br>**krasi** |

Cut out and use ✂

| 3 | 3 |
|---|---|
| **piece** | **here** |
| 3 | 3 |
| **kiosk** | **yesterday** |
| 3 | 3 |
| **this** | **who** |
| 3 | 3 |
| **cheese** | **bad** |
| 3 | 3 |
| **cheap** | **bread** |
| 3 | 3 |
| **wine** | **things** |

Cut out and use ✂

| 4 | 4 |
|---|---|
| **kapios** | **yati** |
| 4 | 4 |
| **ksero** | **randevoo** |
| 4 | 4 |
| **simandiko** | **efxaristo poli** |
| 4 | 4 |
| **thinatos** | **enthiaferon** |
| 4 | 4 |
| **estiatorio** | **apesio** |
| 4 | 4 |
| **arostos/ arosti** | **yatros** |

Cut out and use ✂

| 4 | 4 |
|---|---|
| **why/because** | **someone** |

| 4 | 4 |
|---|---|
| **appointment** | **I know** |

| 4 | 4 |
|---|---|
| **many thanks** | **important** |

| 4 | 4 |
|---|---|
| **interesting** | **possible** |

| 4 | 4 |
|---|---|
| **terrible** | **restaurant** |

| 4 | 4 |
|---|---|
| **doctor** | **sick** |

Cut out and use ✂

| 4 | 4 |
|---|---|
| **psari** | **boro** |
| 4 | 4 |
| **kreas** | **salata** |
| 4 | 4 |
| **nero** | **kanis** |
| 4 | 4 |
| **fisika** | **endaksi** |
| 4 | 4 |
| **kero** | **apopse** |
| 4 | 4 |
| **laxanika** | **kotopoolo** |

| 4 | 4 |
|---|---|
| **I can** | **fish** |
| 4 | 4 |
| **salad** | **meat** |
| 4 | 4 |
| **nobody/ anbody** | **water** |
| 4 | 4 |
| **all right** | **of course** |
| 4 | 4 |
| **tonight** | **time** |
| 4 | 4 |
| **chicken** | **vegetables** |

Cut out and use ✂

| | |
|---|---|
| 5 | 5 |
| **aftokinito** | **nosokomio**<br>**ΝΟΣΟΚΟΜΕΙΟ** |
| 5 | 5 |
| **apagorevete** | **grigora!** |
| 5 | 5 |
| **gramato-**<br>**kivotio** | **isitirio** |
| 5 | 5 |
| **ke ta thio** | **kendrikos**<br>**thromos** |
| 5 | 5 |
| **mera, meres** | **mi-**<br>**kapnizondes** |
| 5 | 5 |
| **moo aresi** | **then moo**<br>**aresi** |

| 5 | 5 |
|---|---|
| **hospital** | **car** |
| **quickly!** | **it's forbidden** |
| **ticket** | **letter box** |
| **main road** | **both (and the two)** |
| **non-smoking** | **day, days** |
| **I don't like** | **I like** |

Cut out and use ✂

| | |
|---|---|
| 5<br><br>**pio** | 5<br><br>**stasi ΣΤΑΣΗ** |
| 5<br><br>**staTHmos<br>ΣΤΑΘΜΟΣ** | 5<br><br>**treno** |
| 5<br><br>**venzinathiko<br>ΒΕΝΖΙΝΑΔΙΚΟ** | 5<br><br>**yemato** |
| 5<br><br>**poli** | 5<br><br>**eki pera** |
| 5<br><br>**proto** | 5<br><br>**ponokefalo** |
| 5<br><br>**astinomia** | 5<br><br>**ipoyio** |

Cut out and use ✂

| 5 (bus) stop | 5 more |
|---|---|
| 5 train | 5 (railway) station |
| 5 full | 5 petrol station |
| 5 over there | 5 city, town |
| 5 headache | 5 first |
| 5 underground | 5 police |

Cut out and use ✂

| | |
|---|---|
| 6<br><br>**aerothromio**<br>**ΑΕΡΟΔΡΟΜΙΟ** | 6<br><br>**mitera** |
| 6<br><br>**Xristooyena** | 6<br><br>**xioni** |
| 6<br><br>**karavi** | 6<br><br>**periptero** |
| 6<br><br>**iperoxos** | 6<br><br>**kserume** |
| 6<br><br>**fandastikos** | 6<br><br>**vivlio** |
| 6<br><br>**sixna** | 6<br><br>**thiamerisma** |

| 6 mother | 6 airport |
| 6 snow | 6 Christmas |
| 6 kiosk | 6 boat |
| 6 we know | 6 wonderful |
| 6 book | 6 fantastic |
| 6 apartment | 6 often |

Cut out and use ✂

| | |
|---|---|
| 6 **ikoyenia** | 6 **meno/emina** |
| 6 **grafo/egrapsa** | 6 **gramata** |
| 6 **pote** | 6 **perimenete!** |
| 6 **karavi** | 6 **vlepo** |
| 6 **protimo** | 6 **kato** |
| 6 **elate!** | 6 **otan** |

| 6 | 6 |
|---|---|
| **I live/I lived** | **family** |
| 6 | 6 |
| **letters** | **I write/I wrote** |
| 6 | 6 |
| **wait!** | **never/ever** |
| 6 | 6 |
| **I see** | **boat** |
| 6 | 6 |
| **down there** | **I prefer** |
| 6 | 6 |
| **when** | **come!** |

Cut out and use ✂

Kalimera, ime o/i... 1

Mia stigmi, parakalo. 1

Pame stin Kerkira. 1

I Patra ine poli omorfi. 1

Thoolevo sto Lonthino. 1

ya tin eteria moo 1

Poo thoolevete? 1

Imaste se thiakopes tora. 1

Exoome ena spiti. 1

Imaste stin Elatha ton Avgoosto. 1

Good morning, I am… 1

A moment, please. 1

We are going to Corfu. 1

Patras is very beautiful. 1

I work in London. 1

for my company 1

Where do you work? 1

We are on holiday now. 1

We have a house. 1

We were in Greece
in August 1

Cut out and use ✂

**Exete thomatio?** 2

**Poo ine to thomatio?** 2

**Poso kostizi?** 2

**Ti ora?** 2

**THeloome na pame stin ATHina.** 2

**stis okto ke misi** 2

**Ine poli akrivo.** 2

**Iparxi ena bar etho?** 2

**kati na fame** 2

**Ton logariasmo, parakalo.** 2

**Do you have a room?** 2

**Where is the room?** 2

**How much does it cost?** 2

**At what time?** 2

**We want (would like) to go to Athens.** 2

**at half past eight** 2

**It is too expensive.** 2

**Is there a bar here?** 2

**something to eat** 2

**The bill, please.** 2

Cut out and use ✂

Pistevo oti...

3

Prepi na pame.

3

THelo na pao ya psonia.

3

Prepi na pao stin trapeza.

3

Mexri pote?

3

Iparxi ena magazi?

3

Then pirazi.

3

Agorasa pola pragmata.

3

Ine poli kalos.

3

konda sto taxithromio

3

I believe that… 3

We must go. 3

I want to go shopping. 3

I must go to the bank. 3

Until when? 3

Is there a shop? 3

It doesn't matter. 3

I have bought a lot of things. 3

He is very nice. 3

near the post office 3

Cut out and use ✂

Iparxi kapios? 4

Then ipe. 4

tin epomeni evthomatha 4

brosta stin porta 4

piso apo tin eklisia 4

Then exoome ora. 4

Pame na fame. 4

Pao mazi too. 4

VoiTHia, parakalo. 4

Pos lene sta Elinika ...? 4

Is there someone?

4

He did not say.

4

next week

4

in front of the door

4

behind the church

4

We don't have time.

4

We are going to eat.

4

I('ll) go with him.

4

Help, please.

4

How do you say... in Greek?

4

Cut out and use ✂

me epistrofi ^5

Lipame, then katalaveno. ^5

Borite na milisete pio arga? ^5

Ti ora exi treno? ^5

Ime poli ikanopioimenos. ^5

Moo aresi to Rover. ^5

Moo aresi yati ine kenooryio. ^5

Moo aresoone ke ta thio. ^5

Then moo aresi to krasi. ^5

Boroome na kapnisoome etho? ^5

return (ticket) 5

I am sorry, I don't understand. 5

Can you speak more slowly? 5

At what time is there a train? 5

I am very satisfied. 5

I like the Rover. 5

I like it because it is new. 5

I like both. 5

I don't like the wine. 5

Can we smoke here? 5

Cut out and use ✂

Kanis then to kseri. <sup>6</sup>

Then to ksero. <sup>6</sup>

Ti simveni? <sup>6</sup>

Ti ipe? <sup>6</sup>

Ti kanoone? <sup>6</sup>

Ti kanete? <sup>6</sup>

Then vlepo... <sup>6</sup>

Then ine tipota. <sup>6</sup>

I ikoyenia moo meni stin Anglia <sup>6</sup>

Pame se ena filo. <sup>6</sup>

Nobody knows it. 6

I don't know it 6

What is the matter? 6

What did he say? 6

What are they doing? 6

How are you? 6

I don't see... 6

There is nothing. 6

My family lives in England. 6

We are going to a friend's. 6

Cut out and use ✂

This is to certify
that

........................................

has successfully completed
a six-week course of

# Fast Greek
# with Elisabeth Smith

with

.....................

results

Date ..............

Author *Elizabeth Smith*

# Praise for Elisabeth Smith

'A language lifeline ... fun, fast and easy.'
(*The Independent*)

'The simple scripts and audio make it crystal clear ... I'm delighted with my progress.'
(*Greece* magazine)

'Its narration is laid-back and encouraging and the method is straightforward. (4-star review)'
(*Time Out*)

'The elements are simple and very straightforward ... strong encouragement ... plenty of opportunity for spoken practice. This course worked very well for me.'
(*Professional Manager* magazine)

'We think it is wonderful.'
(Tom and Maureen Peil, Preston)

'I loved the sense of humour ... Each week I did the final test with bated breath wondering if this time the little bar chart [...] would take a nose dive – but it didn't.'
(Lesly Hopkins, Twickenham)

'This isn't just a package that asks you remember the names for things in a different language this is a package that teaches ... Highly recommended.'
(Maximus)

'It really is an effective way to learn.'
(Mr R. Ellor)

'A solid product offering excellent value for money ... a great place to start.'
(A. M. Boughey)

'One of the best courses around to get you that little bit further than the basics.'
(Johannsen Krister)

**more...**

'The words are very clearly spoken and the form of presentation witty and lively to keep your interest, and clever choice of subject matter also keep learning interesting and aid memory. This is a very strong language course and I recommend it.'
(vh1967)

'The Elisabeth Smith courses are a superb resource for the learner who needs to be able to speak the language in a short period of time and with a good degree of understanding.'
(Will Boyce)

'I was surprised at what I'd achieved after this course and recommend it.'

'This is an absolute must have ... You'll be so glad you bought it!'
(Elodie)

Now join me on:

Facebook at www.facebook.com/elisabethsmithlanguages

Twitter at www.twitter.com/LanguagesESmith